# GROWTH AND POLICY IN DEVELOPING COUNTRIES

INITIATIVE FOR POLICY DIALOGUE AT COLUMBIA UNIVERSITY

THE INITIATIVE FOR POLICY
DIALOGUE AT COLUMBIA UNIVERSITY

JOSÉ ANTONIO OCAMPO AND
JOSEPH E. STIGLITZ, SERIES EDITORS

Other titles published by Columbia University Press in this series:

*Escaping the Resource Curse*, Macartan Humphreys,
Jeffrey D. Sachs, and Joseph E. Stiglitz, eds.

*The Right to Know*, Ann Florini, ed.

*Privatization: Successes and Failures*, Gérard Roland, ed.

# GROWTH AND POLICY IN DEVELOPING COUNTRIES

## A Structuralist Approach

José Antonio Ocampo,
Codrina Rada, and Lance Taylor

(with contributions from Mariángela Parra)

Columbia University Press

NEW YORK

Columbia University Press
*Publishers Since 1893*
New York   Chichester, West Sussex
Copyright © 2009 Columbia University Press
All rights reserved

Library of Congress Cataloging-in-Publication Data

Ocampo, José Antonio.
   Growth and policy in developing countries : a structuralist approach / José
Antonio Ocampo, Codrina Rada, and Lance Taylor ; (with contributions from Maria
Ángela Parra).
       p.   cm. — (Initiative for policy dialogue)
   Includes bibliographical references and index.
   ISBN 978-0-231-15014-9 (cloth : alk. paper) — ISBN 978-0-231-52083-6 (ebook)
   1. Economic development—Developing countries.   2. Developing countries—Eco-
nomic policy.   I. Rada, Codrina.   II. Taylor, Lance, 1940–   III. Title.   IV. Series.

HC59.7.O263 2009
338.9009172'4—dc22

                                                              2009025303

Columbia University Press books are printed on permanent and durable acid-free paper.

This book is printed on paper with recycled content.

Printed in the United States of America

c 10 9 8 7 6 5 4 3 2 1

# The Initiative for Policy Dialogue at Columbia

## JOSÉ ANTONIO OCAMPO AND
## JOSEPH E. STIGLITZ, SERIES EDITORS

THE INITIATIVE FOR POLICY DIALOGUE (IPD) at Columbia University brings together academics, policy makers, and practitioners from developed and developing countries to address the most pressing issues in economic policy today. IPD is an important part of Columbia's broad program on development and globalization. The Initiative for Policy Dialogue at Columbia: Challenges in Development and Globalization presents the latest academic thinking on a wide range of development topics and lays out alternative policy options and trade-offs. Written in a language accessible to policy makers and students alike, this series is unique in that it both shapes the academic research agenda and furthers the economic policy debate, facilitating a more democratic discussion of development policies.

Given the fact that economic growth is one of the major determinants of living standards, one the major concerns of IPD has been to understand why so many developing countries have failed to grow rapidly in recent decades. This implies a critical look at why policy recommendations, particularly those emanating from the Washington Consensus, now in demise, failed to do so. This book looks at this issue from a structuralist perspective. Structuralists conduct a system-wide analysis, looking at a wide range of factors that affect an economy's strength and stability: its position in the global economic system, its production and trade patterns, its financial structure and how it limits its macroeconomic policy space, and its social structures.

The book begins with a survey of Structuralist methods and post-WWII trends in global economic growth. It then discusses the role that patterns in productivity, production structures, and capital accumulation play in the growth dynamics of developing countries. The book next outlines the evolution of trade patterns and the effect of terms of trade on the economic performance of developing countries, especially those that are dependent on commodity exports. A chapter on the structural limits of macroeconomic policy highlights the negative impact of financial volatility and certain financial structures, and recommends policies that better manage the external shocks that developing economies face. These policies are further developed in a section concentrating specifically on growth and structural improvements. In a concluding chapter, the book determines which policy options—macro, industrial, or commercial—best fit in different kinds of developing economies.

This book hopes to answer the needs of those doing research on growth and development as well as of policy makers around the developing world at a time of major uncertainties. The book is relatively short and we hope that it will be used as a textbook in courses on development economics and macroeconomics for developing countries. It is accessible to those with a less technical background, undergraduate students, and the general reader, without compromising the rigor of economic analysis by including the technical material in the appendices to the relevant chapters.

For more information about IPD's activities and its upcoming books, visit www.policydialogue.org

*To Raúl Prebisch and Hollis Chenery,*
*pioneers of structuralism*

# Contents

# Figures

# Tables

# Preface

IN THIS BOOK, we address growth and development strategies in the developing world (including the so-called emerging and transition economies) based on the structuralist tradition of economic thought. Structuralist views of how an economy works and especially how developing countries can advance toward economic and social sustainability have long been an integral part of economics in general and of development economics in particular. The appeal of structuralist economics to policy makers and researchers follows from its system-wide approach, including the social context in which economies operate. We believe that structuralism provides the best way to understand the problems people in poor countries have to confront in trying to reshape their national economies.

There is, however, no comprehensive text that looks at growth and development from this perspective, in both empirical and analytical terms, comparable to the diverse supply of mainstream texts on economic growth. In this book, we try to fill this gap by using structuralist methods to analyze the economic performance of developing countries around the world since the 1960s.

Traditionally, structuralist economists begin their analysis with a look at "stylized facts" that characterize the economy. The starting point in this book is the observed divergence in the economic performance between industrial and developing countries, and among the latter since the 1960s but particularly following the oil and interest rate shocks of the late 1970s. Our main task is to ascertain reasons why relatively few countries have managed to grow steadily for long time periods. Understanding, in turn, how the structure of the economic system, institutions, and the stage of financial development can constrain policy space is essential in providing the right solutions to policy problems as they arise in developing countries.

The structuralist approach departs from the orthodox policy framework proposed since the 1970s by mainstream economists and international financial institutions such as the World Bank and the International Monetary Fund. Now, after more than three decades of negligible success, the influence of mainstream views on policy strategies and policy making in the developing world is clearly in decline. However, the void, in both academic and non-academic economic literature, in terms of analysis and a coherent set of policy alternatives, remains present.

From this perspective, this book is very timely and will answer the needs of those doing research on growth and development as well as of policy makers around the developing world. The book is relatively short, and we hope that it will be used as a textbook for courses on development economics and macroeconomics in developing countries. It is accessible to those with a less technical background, undergraduate students, and the general reader, without compromising the rigor of economic analysis by including the technical material in the appendices to the relevant chapters.

## The Structure of the Book

Chapter 1 starts with an overall presentation of structuralist views on development and the role of the state. It also provides a first look at the policy issues that the book analyzes, in the context of the broader debates on development and, in this sense, provides a summary of the major issues raised throughout the book.

Chapters 2 to 5 are empirical in character. They present major stylized facts about developing countries' economic performance.

Chapter 2 summarizes the post–World War II history of economic growth. The general message is that after the "golden age" of rapid worldwide economic expansion, there was a "great divergence" in the late twentieth century[1] both between industrial and developing countries, and among the latter. This divergence was associated with major international shocks in interest rates and commodity terms of trade, the effects of which lasted for almost a quarter of a century. The early twenty-first century saw again broad-based growth in the developing world, which hit the wall as a result of the global financial meltdown of 2007–2008.

Chapter 3 first takes up patterns of productivity growth and other supply side factors. It is shown that sustained growth in "successful" regions was accompanied by structural changes including output and labor share shifts toward industry and modern services, which is therefore the main determinant of sustained productivity growth. Variations in labor underemployment also play an important role, providing the labor force that dynamic modern sectors require but also absorbing in informal activities the labor surplus not employed in industry and modern services. In turn, capital stock and output growth rates are also related, possibly due to demand rather than supply-side causality.

In contrast, greater education and foreign direct investment are not closely tied to growth. There was a considerable variation in energy use patterns across regions, but in all cases the energy/labor ratio did not fall.

Chapter 4 is devoted to international trade and associated structural changes. Overall the chapter highlights that economic growth seems to be associated more with *how* an economy integrates itself into the global markets rather than with trade openness per se. Specifically, fast-growing economies have usually moved toward manufactured exports with high technological content and, to a lesser extent, mid- and low-technology manufactures. The stagnating economies tended to remain exporters of primary products and natural resource-based manufactures.

Chapter 5 considers the ways different net borrowing flows among different economic agents relate to each other. Neither the widely accepted "twin external/ fiscal deficits" nor the "consumption-smoothing" views of macro adjustment seem to apply. The most typical pattern is parallel movements of *private* and external deficits. This pattern implies that the business cycle is dominated in developing countries by pro-cyclical swings in private spending (investment and consumption) that closely interact with—and, in fact, are largely determined by—pro-cyclical capital flows.

The rest of the book (chapters 6 to 9) presents simple structuralist models and analytical frameworks that help to make these stylized facts understandable and that draw upon them for basic recommendations on macroeconomic and development policies.

The discussion begins in chapter 6 with a review of how different financial structures can constrain—and, in contrast, how financial development facilitates—policy choice. It also shows how different financial structures generate opportunities for financial speculation and associated macroeconomic instability. From this analysis, basic ideas about financial development and regulation are sketched out.

Chapter 7 sets up a three-gap framework that facilitates understanding of the interaction between net borrowing patterns of different economic agents in developing countries. This framework serves as the basis for the analysis of counter-cyclical macroeconomic policies (fiscal, monetary, and foreign exchange rate and reserve management) and supporting capital management techniques (regulations on cross-border capital flows and counter-cyclical prudential regulation). The chapter ends with an analysis of the impacts of foreign aid on low-income countries.

Policies regarding growth and structural development strategies are the focus of Chapter 8. The basic framework is a model in which the interaction between supply and demand factors generates a dual link between economic growth and productivity improvements. Variations in underemployment (in the "reserve army of the underemployed," as we call it in the book) are essential in this dynamic, reflecting the crucial role played by structural underemployment in "dual economies," in which an informal low-productivity sector coexists with a modern sector subject to increasing returns, a structural characteristic of developing countries. Policy frameworks for industry, agriculture, and trade are drawn from this analysis.

Finally, chapter 9 summarizes the main stylized facts presented throughout the book as well as policy options—macro, industrial, and commercial—with a focus on what sorts of interventions fit best in different kinds of developing economies.

We should note that the sequence of the analytical chapters, which covers from the short- to the long-term determinants of economic growth, is the inverse of that followed in the empirical chapters. This structure actually makes sense, as the empirical analysis starts with the focus on the central motivation of the book, the sharply different rates of growth among countries, whereas the analytical part follows the traditional sequence of macroeconomics textbooks, from the short to the long run. One interesting feature of this structure is that the main motivation of the book, explaining growth divergence among countries, figures prominently at the start and the end of the book.

## Acknowledgments

Earlier, versions of chapters 2 and 3 were originally written for the United Nations Department of Economic and Social Affairs in preparation of the *World Economic and Social Survey 2006*, a revised version of which was later published as *Uneven Economic Development* (Ocampo and Vos 2008). Mariángela Parra co-authored two chapters, and Rob Vos provided very helpful inputs at all stages along the way to the present volume. Jaime Ros also carefully read and provided comments to a first draft of the book that were very useful in preparing the final version.

## Notes

1. This "great divergence" of the late twentieth century may be seen as part of the divergence between now rich and poor countries that has taken place since the industrial revolution—the longer time period for which authors such as Pomeranz (2000) have used this concept.

GROWTH AND POLICY IN DEVELOPING COUNTRIES

# CHAPTER 1

# Economic Structure, Policy, and Growth

ALMOST A DECADE into the twenty-first century, absolute poverty still pervades outside the industrialized world. Helping poor people in developing countries improve their standards of living is on the short list of international policy goals. There are a multitude of ideas about how poverty should be analyzed and attacked. Although there have been some success stories, particularly in East Asia, the unhappy truth is that anti-poverty programs in developing countries have quite often failed or have had limited success.[1]

The reason is that they did not enable poor economies to generate long-term growth of real per capita income. A useful rule of thumb is that developing and transition economies should sustain at least 2 percent annual per capita real growth of gross domestic product (GDP). This would stop the gap separating their standards of living from the industrial world's from widening even further, and 3 percent or more would gradually reduce it. A 2 percent per capita growth rate can make a big dent in poverty by increasing average income by 22 percent over 10 years and 49 percent over 20. In addition, growth can only address poverty concerns if it generates new jobs to keep pace with a rising labor force.

Relatively few developing and transition economies have been able to mount steady growth at 2 percent or higher for long time periods. The quarter century or so after the second oil and interest rate shocks of 1979 was particularly critical in this regard, as many developing countries started to face long-term stagnation or even regression. Our task in this book is to ascertain the reasons and to suggest policy initiatives to offset the difficulties that we will uncover. Our focus is the links between economic *structure*, policy, and growth. The emphasis on the term "structure" is essential, as our analysis is deeply embedded in a "structuralist" tradition of development economics, which we view as providing the best way to understand the problems that the people in poor countries have to confront in trying to reshape their national economies.

Since the mid-1970s and, particularly, the 1980s and under the strong influence of the World Bank and the International Monetary Fund, there was a significant change in the overall framework for development policies, from the tradition of strong state intervention that had prevailed after World War II toward what came to be called the "Washington consensus." This orthodox framework asserts that economic liberalization—that is, letting the market take over from the state—is the answer to speeding up growth in the developing world. This recommendation was followed, to a greater or lesser extent, in developing and transition economies, and they experienced a poor growth record.

Our framework departs from these orthodox views, arguing in particular that there is clearly something missing from mainstream analysis: *it omits structure and structural change*. This argument may sound paradoxical because the main orthodox slogan was "structural reform," the term frequently used instead of "economic liberalization," which is what it was meant to imply. The use of the term "structural" in these programs is entirely different from the older usage adhered to in this book and explained later in this chapter.

Poverty is central to this distinction. The most widely publicized antipoverty program today is the Millennium Development Goals (MDG) effort sponsored by the United Nations. It calls for roughly doubling foreign aid to the poorest economies over the next 10 years. The aims are exemplary. An incomplete list of the MDGs ranges from halving by 2015 the levels of extreme poverty and hunger that developing countries had in 1990, providing universal primary education, sharply reducing infant and maternal mortality, increasing access to water and sanitation, and ensuring environmental sustainability.

We certainly accept these merit social goals, but present two caveats. First, there is a major question about whether foreign aid flows will increase from around $100 billion per year in 2007 to the levels required to meet the MDGs. This problem is compounded by the fact that the measured aid flows include "debt relief" to the poorest countries, which is not really new aid, as well as technical assistance delivered by professionals from donor countries, which may be useful but is very costly. Such outlays are not really funds available for the recipient countries to spend on achieving the MDGs.

Second, the emphasis on merit social goals hides the fact that the key to reducing poverty is growth of the purchasing power of the poor. As discussed in chapter 7, international aid by itself is unlikely to make sustained growth in the poorest economies come about. Growth accompanied and supported by structural change is what is needed.

How economic policy can be utilized in diverse structural circumstances to generate growth is the question at hand. The complications to be addressed are summarized in this chapter, which serves as an introduction to the chapters to come.

## Economic Growth

To begin, we should define the terms "economic structure," "policy," and "growth." The latter is measured in traditional fashion as an increase in real gross domestic product (GDP; either as a level or per capita), both economy-wide and for specific productive sectors.

## *Measuring Economic Output*

The basic idea about GDP measurement comes from John Maynard Keynes (1936). In his *General Theory*, he explicitly embraced double-entry bookkeeping for the entire economy by postulating that national income=national output. As discussed later, in an economy hypothetically closed to foreign trade, an equivalent assertion is that saving=investment. For Keynes, investment was the driving force with saving adjusting to meet it via changes in the level of output.

National accounting had been proposed many times before, but Keynes was the first to adopt income and output as joint measures of economic value (Mirowski 1989). The national income and product accounts—or "national accounts," for short—can be extended to incorporate mutually offsetting financial transactions in the flows of funds accounts, which add up over time to national financial balance sheets. "National balance sheets" refer only to the assets and liabilities of residents in a country vis-à-vis residents in the rest of the world; it is in this sense that we will use the term. Asset and liability positions do not usually offset each other, giving rise to a situation in which there are either net national foreign assets (the residents of the country are net investors in the rest of the world) or net foreign liabilities, the more common situation in the developing world (and in the United States, with some developing countries now being net lenders).

In the simplest version of the national accounts, the value of output is equal to the sum of all forms of spending: private consumption, investment, government spending, and exports. Producing the output generates income flows which go to workers, recipients of profit incomes, proprietors such as peasant farmers and small merchants, and the rest of the world (via imports into the local economy and transfers such as profit remittances going out). Much of macroeconomics is about rules to determine how the system adjusts to bring equality between income (or output) and spending. Examples are presented throughout this book.

The double entries suggest that GDP can be calculated as a sum of either incomes or spending. Most advanced economies do it both ways and report a "discrepancy" (usually in the neighborhood of 1 percent) between the two sets of estimates. Many poor countries attempt only the output side and compute some component of spending (usually private consumption) as a "residual."

Sectoral output or "value-added" estimates themselves may be residuals as well, each computed as a total value of gross output minus costs of intermediate inputs.[2] GDP from the output side is the sum of levels of value-added across economic activities. Value-added in turn should be the sum of payments to "primary factors of production" such as labor, capital, and entrepreneurship—that is, incomes.

GDP estimates are blends of diverse economic indicators of varying reliability mixed into one overall system of accounts. The cooking procedures differ greatly across countries and time. However, for better or worse, economic policy discussion is always framed nowadays in terms of the national accounts.

GDP must be estimated using current market prices. "Real" GDP is such an estimate at current prices divided by some price index,[3] in principle constructed in such a way as to be consistent with the overall accounting framework. Numbers on economic growth are always based on real output computed in this fashion. In turn, if total GDP is growing at a rate of, say, 4 percent per year, real per capita GDP must be growing at 4 percent minus the rate of population growth.

A related concept is average "productivity" or real output divided by some real input, say, a measure of labor, capital, or energy employed in production. Estimates of labor come from employment statistics, capital is the sum of levels of real net investment (gross fixed capital formation less depreciation) over time. Productivity growth is the growth rate of output minus the growth rate of the relevant input. Much of the discussion to follow (in chapter 3 in particular) centers on different measures of productivity growth.

## Supply-Side Considerations

Growth rates of labor and capital productivity are the numbers most commonly considered. Income per capita cannot increase without rising labor productivity, but what about capital? For most economies, the evidence suggests that the output/capital ratio is fairly stable (as it is across business cycles in the United States) or else tends to fall. Four observations follow:

First, using simple algebra (see appendix 3.2), one can show that the ratio of capital productivity to labor productivity must be equal to the ratio of employed labor to employed capital. During recent economic growth in East Asia, the labor/capital ratio decreased because of the high rate of investment in those economies. With labor productivity growth rates well over 2 percent per year, the equation just mentioned shows that, based on a "theorem of accounting," capital productivity either had to fall or stagnate. Critics of the East Asian development model stress that it is "inefficient" because of falling capital productivity. The assertion is meaningless, because it turns an algebraic artifact into a diagnosis of economic malaise. The same empty accusations apply to many developed economies such as Japan, the United States, or the United Kingdom during their years of fast growth, as they all experienced falling or stagnating capital productivity (see table 2.8 in Foley and Michl 1999).

Second, mainstream economists put a great deal of emphasis on "total factor productivity growth" (TFPG) as proposed by Robert Solow (1957). TFPG is a weighted average of labor and capital productivity growth rates, with the weights being the shares in value-added of payments to providers of labor and capital. The problem is that the weights are virtually impossible to compute in developing economies. There the data typically show that labor remunerations may be somewhere around 20–40 percent of GDP in low- to middle-income economies, with recognizable payments to capital in a similar range. The rest, calculated by employing the residual approach, goes to "proprietors" such as peasant farmers and urban service providers. What fractions of their incomes should be attributed to capital (including land) and labor is very difficult to say. It is better to look at trends in labor and capital productivity separately to try to figure things out.

Third, the standard approach, devised by Frank Ramsey (1928) and Solow (1956), is to explain output growth solely from the side of supply, stressing the "contributions" of TFPG plus labor and capital growth rates to the total. The capital stock grows as a result of each year's flow of investment, assumed to be determined by available saving under conditions of full employment.[4] Labor supply is supposed to be set by demographic developments. TFPG follows from unspecified "technological factors."

An alternative view is that, for reasons discussed later in this chapter, labor productivity is likely to grow more rapidly when output growth accelerates (and perhaps when real wages rise, inducing firms to use labor inputs more effectively). Output itself may be driven by increases in demand when labor is not fully employed and, in particular, not fully employed in the "modern" sector of the economy. This situation is typical in developing countries, where a large "subsistence" labor force in "traditional" rural and "informal" urban activities exists alongside the "modern" sectors of the economy, as emphasized by Lewis (1954).

Under these conditions, a demand push generated by external or domestic factors will increase productivity growth, by allowing dynamic modern sectors to draw upon subsistence labor—which, using the analogy proposed by Karl Marx, operates as a sort of "reserve army," but of the underemployed rather than the unemployed. Shifting labor from low- to high-productivity activities will by itself lead to an increase in labor productivity, but this effect is compounded by the fact that, as we will see later, a faster rate in the growth of production in the modern sector will lead to productivity improvements. Faster productivity  growth is therefore the joint effect of the reduction of underemployment and improvements in productivity generated by dynamic growth in the modern sector. On the other hand, if demand is weak, the economy will adapt through the absorption of the surplus labor by traditional and informal activities, thus generating a reduction in overall labor productivity.

Under these conditions, weak productivity performance is the *result* rather than the *cause* of weak output and demand growth. More generally, output and productivity growth rates are jointly determined. Employment growth then follows as the difference between them. It may fall short of the expansion of the labor force, or even lead to a situation of "jobless growth."

In a successful development experience, employment growth in the modern sector should exceed the growth of the total labor force, thus allowing increasing absorption of the underemployed into higher productivity activities. But the opposite may also happen, not just because growth is weak but also because the economy is structurally predisposed toward jobless growth. This situation is not uncommon in mineral exporting economies where the most dynamic sectors create very few jobs or during trade liberalization episodes when firms facing rising external competition increase productivity at the micro level basically by shedding workers.

This reading of the evidence, introduced by Nicholas Kaldor (1978, chap. 4 based on a lecture from 1966) is used extensively in chapter 8. According to Kaldor's analysis, physical capital serves as one of the major vehicles for bringing new technologies into the system with its growth ultimately regulated by the growth rate of investment demand and saving adjusting via change in output as suggested by Keynes. Higher investment leads to productivity increases as it incorporates new technologies and product innovations (Kaldor 1978, chaps. 1 and 2). Output expansion in turn generates productivity increases through the exploitation of static and dynamic economies of scale, associated in the latter case with learning-by-doing and technological innovations induced by production experience.

Labor underemployment thus allows investment dynamics to play the leading role in determining the rate of growth of both GDP and productivity. In open economies, the determining demand factor may be exports or external financing. These two variables play a crucial role in macroeconomic dynamics in developing countries. Interestingly, as we will see, they are also key determinants of aggregate supply when foreign exchange becomes scare.

As is often the case in macroeconomics, the data do not suffice to distinguish between the theories, but there may be a presumption in favor of the demand-oriented analysis when we see major variations in underemployment. In any case, the traditional supply-oriented interpretation does not seem to hold in developing countries. When supply constraints are important, it is generally foreign exchange rather than the capital stock or the available labor force that plays the crucial role.

What the data can certainly do, as we will see in chapter 3, is rule out any strong association between other supply-side factors, such as increases in average years of schooling ("human capital accumulation") and high levels of direct foreign investment, with the growth rate of per capita income.

Finally, under the threat of global warming, energy use from fossil fuels is of growing policy concern. As with capital, one can show that the growth rate of labor productivity must be equal to the growth rate of energy productivity plus the growth rate of the energy/labor ratio.

The ratio of fossil fuel energy use to labor ranges from 0.49 terajoules per person-year in industrialized economies (0.61 in the United States) to 0.01 in sub-Saharan Africa (SSA).[5] Between 1990 and 2004, energy/labor ratios were growing at rates exceeding 3 percent per year in the rapidly growing Asian economies. In industrialized countries, the ratio grew at 0.1 percent after decreasing by –0.3 percent per year between 1970 and 1990 (see full details in chapter 3).

Rough calculations using a study on carbon dioxide emissions by climate experts (Socolow and Pacala 2006) suggest that to hold global greenhouse gas emissions constant, developing country energy/labor ratios might have to *decrease* by 1 percent per year.[6] Whether such a shift in energy use patterns will be even remotely possible, without seriously undermining efforts to increase productivity, is very much an open question.

## Economic Structure

The concept of "economic structure" refers to the composition of production activities, the associated patterns of specialization in international trade, the technological capabilities of the economy, including the educational level of the labor force, the structure of ownership of factors of production, the nature and development of basic state institutions, and the degree of development and constraints under which certain markets operate (the absence of certain segments of the financial market or the presence of a large underemployed labor force, for example).

These basic factors are reflected in relationships among the numbers that appear in the national, trade, fiscal, monetary, and financial accounts along with indicators of employment, educational levels, and energy use. They are also reflected in the network of production and demand linkages among sectors in an economy—both backward and forward linkages in Hirschman's (1958) well-known terminology—or, indeed, the lack or destruction of them.

Some of these relationships have important distributive implications. In this case, structuralists adopt the "classical" approach of Adam Smith, David Ricardo, Thomas Malthus, and Karl Marx in focusing on collective actors—organized groups or classes such as capitalists, landlords, and peasants. Relationships among collective actors help to determine the way both state and market institutions are framed, which in turn influence relative prices and the income distribution (think of Malthus's theory of population and Marx's reserve army of the unemployed), as well as technical progress, investment, and aggregate supply. On the other sides of markets are factors that determine the level of effective demand ("animal spirits" of investing firms for Keynes) and also the pace of productivity growth. As in Kaldor's model previously sketched, the economy's position depends on these interacting "supply" and "demand" systems.

Contemporary structuralists also follow Keynes in emphasizing how accounting restrictions among economic actors—essentially, what is bought must be sold (the gist of the national accounts system) or what is borrowed must be lent (the flows of funds accounts)—play a crucial role in determining how aggregate demand and supply forces interact.

Such macroeconomic accounting balances underlie Keynes's basic insight that often, but not always, the level of effective demand determines aggregate supply. As we have pointed out, in a developing country this rule most often breaks down when there are strict limits on available foreign exchange.

Underlying both demand and supply are also shifting financial decisions by collective actors such as the real estate and stock market speculators and hedge funds that can strongly affect the overall outcome. The external crises described in the following sections are telling examples. The economy's financial structure strongly influences the ebb and flow of transactions within it.

As will be clear throughout this book, a critical structural issue for developing countries is their trade and financial linkages with the rest of the world—their "insertion" into the world economy, to use the terminology of Latin American structuralism. This insertion is influenced, in turn, by the structure of the global economy, and the particular "asymmetries" that characterize it—its "center-periphery" dimensions, to use again the terminology from this influential group of structuralists.

Two sorts of asymmetries are particularly important in this regard: (1) most technology generation is concentrated in industrial countries, which determines the direction of technology flows but also the patterns of specialization in the production of goods and services with different technological content; and (2) the world currencies are the currencies of the major international economic powers, international financial intermediation is concentrated in those countries, and developing countries are either cut off entirely from those capital flows or are subject to strong upward and downward swings in the availability and costs of external financing (Ocampo and Martin 2003).[7]

## Production Structure and Growth

There are two views regarding the role and implications of production structure for growth. The conventional narrative is that structural change in the patterns of production, expressed numerically in terms of variations in sectoral contributions to output, employment, investment, and patterns of specialization, is just a side effect of growth. As the economy expands and markets enlarge, new demands require new production processes that come into being by attracting inputs such as labor and capital. The structural configuration adjusts to incorporate novel activities or to enlarge existing ones. Growing economies almost always move from primary to secondary and further toward tertiary sectors.

The alternative view is that these patterns of structural change are not just a byproduct of growth but rather are among the prime movers. This has inherent policy implications. Because production structure must change if growth and development are to proceed, conscious choice of policies that will drive the transformation of the system toward certain sectors is essential for long-term economic expansion.

This insight is ignored by most contemporary economic theory. But it arises from observation and analysis of economic performance of developing countries around the world in the past and present. Economists who have been trained within the structuralist tradition share this perspective, holding that development requires economic transformation or the "ability of an economy to constantly generate new dynamic activities" (Ocampo 2005), particularly those characterized by higher productivity and increasing returns to scale of production as reflected in decreasing costs per unit of output. This logic underlies Kaldor's growth model, which was previously described and will be discussed further in chapter 8.

One key aspect of growth in the poorest countries is that agriculture dominates the economy. Therefore, agricultural productivity growth is crucial, as in sub-Saharan Africa now. But productivity increases in the sector are significantly constrained by lack of access to modern technology, natural factors such as low fertility land, and mostly by its intrinsic inability to offer increasing returns. Hence, per capita output growth at 2 percent requires even higher growth rates of labor productivity in leading sectors (assuming that the ratio of employed labor to the population is fairly stable).

At higher income levels, the leading sector(s) must offer increasing returns and opportunities for robust output growth in response to demand. As demonstrated in chapter 3 and a raft of historical studies, a clear pattern of structural change emerges from the data for economies (today mostly in East and South Asia) which sustain rapid growth. Historically, manufacturing has almost always served as the engine for productivity growth but not for job creation (India with its information processing boom is an intriguing recent exception). For a sector or the entire economy to generate employment, its per capita growth rate of demand has to exceed its productivity growth. Net job creation usually takes place in services.

As discussed in chapter 4, patterns of international trade also shift as economies grow richer. Their exports become more technically sophisticated and shift from raw materials toward manufactured products, especially in recent decades with the explosion of assembly manufacturing around the world. Import composition also shifts in response to overall changes in the basic structure of the economy. Indeed, those changes in the pattern of specialization in international trade are an essential part of the transformation of production structures, a fact that has been highlighted by the role that the terms "import substitution" and "export diversification" have played in development debates. Concerning these changes, one key question is whether an economy can pass through the raw material and assembly export stages to sell products abroad that have a high value-added content at home.

## Development Policy

The links between growth and production and trade structures have profound implications for development policy. There is an insight that was placed at the center of development writing from the 1940s to the 1960s but can be traced to before Adam Smith. It has been recently restated by Reinert (2006) and formalized by Ros (2000) and Rada (2007), following classical development economics and Kaldor, respectively, as well as the essentials of Lewis's labor surplus model. It says that the economy can be viewed usefully as a combination of increasing returns sectors and more plodding constant or decreasing returns activities.[8] Dynamics between markets, forces of innovation, finance, and productive sectors can produce virtuous circles of growth and development based on decreasing costs per unit output. Smith realized but did not emphasize that the invisible hand may need assistance in promoting the development of such virtuous circles. As Alexander Hamilton and Friedrich List pointed out explicitly a few years later, the conscious action (the visible hand) of the policy maker is often required.

The goal is to stimulate the sectors with increasing returns while shifting resources from elsewhere in the economy. The patterns of productivity and employment growth sketched previously and presented in detail in chapter 3 precisely represent this sort of structural change. The now-industrialized economies succeeded at this task. The question is how to design policies that will facilitate similar processes elsewhere. Historically, the state has played a crucial role.

For many decades, there was proactive developmentalist state intervention in the now-industrialized economies (Chang 2002) and in twentieth-century success cases in the developing world (Amsden 2003). Consider the United States in the nineteenth century. Booming agricultural exports prevented a foreign exchange bottleneck. There were enormous public subsidies (with enormous corruption) to support investment in canals and railroads and the highest tariffs in the world to protect industry. Entrepreneurs from John D. Rockefeller to the "Robber Barons"[9] abounded, paying scant heed to conventional property rights (if only because they had well-remunerated judges under their control).

For many developing countries, possibilities of pursuing any such strategy effectively disappeared in the last two decades of the twentieth century with the metastasis of the Washington consensus. Under the tutelage of World Bank and International Monetary Fund, countries moved to liberalize their external current and capital accounts along with domestic financial and (to a lesser extent) labor markets. They also privatized public enterprises, de-emphasized or many times entirely dismantled industrial policy interventions, and allowed a greater private sector role in general. Fiscal austerity figured in many programs sponsored by the Bretton Woods Institutions.

In effect, policy makers in developing countries had their hands tied by the liberalization process—in the areas of macroeconomics and industrial policy among others. In a currently popular phrase, their "policy space" contracted immensely. One task for the future is to devise institutional changes that can open it back up. Suggestions are presented throughout the book.

## Foreign Exchange Constraints and Financial Structures

Structural factors relevant to the growth process are not limited to production and the forms of insertion into the global economy. Constraints on macroeconomic policy are also very important. The two most critical constraints relate to external and domestic financing.

As already pointed out, the limited availability of hard currency is perhaps the crucial bottleneck for many developing countries at different stages of their development process because it can hold down both supply and demand. The lack of foreign exchange during economic downturns, due to falling export revenues or reduced access to external financing, forces authorities many times to adopt macroeconomic policies that end up reducing economic activity and employment. On the contrary, if foreign exchange were readily available, effective demand could increase and it would stimulate private sector investment and innovation. How to relax the foreign exchange constraint has therefore been a perennial preoccupation for the economic authorities in developing country capitals almost everywhere.

Domestic finance is needed to support investment in both working and fixed capital. However, commercial banks in many developing countries do not provide even necessary working capital, particularly for small firms, and are particularly bad at providing long-term financing for new fixed capital formation.

For this reason, the state has frequently had to step in to provide financing, often through the vehicle of development banks targeting productive investment.

The development of local financial capital markets—stock and bond markets and associated transactions in derivatives—is also limited in many developing countries, a fact that has major implications for running both fiscal and monetary policy. If there is no adequate way to finance public sector deficits by selling treasury bonds in the domestic capital market, authorities may force commercial banks to buy them or resort directly to central bank financing, thus generating a complex and undesirable interaction between fiscal deficits and money creation.

Furthermore, most advanced forms of monetary policy depend critically on the existence of a domestic capital market in which the central bank can actively sell and buy bonds. Macroeconomic policy is significantly constrained by the availability of instruments when there is no developed domestic capital market. This issue is discussed extensively in chapter 6.

## Macroeconomic Environment and Growth

A supportive macroeconomic environment for growth is essential. The details have varied greatly in successful countries, but a few general observations apply. They are developed in more detail in chapter 7. The key point is that there can be structural limitations on policy freedom in developing countries, even before restrictions that donors and international financial institutions may impose.

Supposing that growth of production and employment is the major policy goal, then "macro" prices, in particular the real exchange rate, should not be "too low"[10] and the real interest rate should not be "too high." Low, positive real interest rates stimulate investment and help balance the financial system. A weak ("high") exchange rate holds imports down and helps an economy push into new export lines. Stability of macro prices is also desirable. If they fluctuate rapidly, medium-term business planning is impossible. In practice, maintaining a favorable configuration of macro prices is generally not an easy task.

"External balance" is also a key issue. Suppose for concreteness that an economy is running a current account deficit (that is, exports and current payments from abroad such as emigrant remittances are less than imports plus payments such as interest and profit remittances going out). The economy must borrow externally to cover the deficit (even most foreign aid is conventionally treated as loans). Incoming new lending from the rest of the world is positive.[11]

Moreover, some group(s) within the economy must be doing the counterpart borrowing to match this lending from abroad. The simplest separation is between the public and private sectors—one or the other or both must be running a deficit to absorb financial capital inflows from abroad. In other words, private expenditure minus income (or investment minus saving) plus the consolidated government deficit must equal the foreign deficit.

Finally, as discussed extensively in the following chapters, unstable external financing plays a crucial role in the determination of macroeconomic balances and dynamics in developing countries. A major challenge is that macroeconomic policies are pushed toward behaving in a "pro-cyclical" way. That is, they reinforce both the boom and the crisis, and thus magnify the effects of external oscillations on the domestic economy. Macroeconomic policy space is limited by one of the very factors that determine the business cycle: unstable capital flows (Stiglitz et al. 2006).

As will be seen, the interplay among macro prices, external balance, and pro-cyclicality can be quite complex and strongly conditions possibilities for economic growth. Two illustrative scenarios help to make this point: external shocks and unstable international capital flows.

## External Shocks

After an external crisis generated by reduced export earnings or limited external financing (in many cases these two macroeconomic shocks coincide), an economy almost always is forced to cut its external deficit or increase its surplus. Since net borrowing from abroad must fall or even become negative, the domestic private and public sectors have to cut back their borrowing or become net lenders. The private sector can curtail consumption and investment, and the government can slash spending and raise taxes. The economy goes into recession and may take a very long time to recover. The "lost decade" in Latin America after the debt crisis that erupted around 1980 is a striking example, as illustrated in chapter 2. Based on an empirical analysis of net-borrowing flows in chapter 5, a three-gap model devised to analyze such contingencies is presented in chapter 7.

There is also a risk if too much foreign exchange comes in. A spending-led output boom can occur with no expansion of productive capacity. One example is the Ivory Coast, the World Bank's poster child of the 1970s that thereafter became a disaster. Economists talk about a "Dutch disease" with big drops in domestic productive activity in wake of a foreign exchange bonanza. (The phrase was coined by the *Economist* magazine in 1977 in reference to deindustrialization after natural gas discoveries in The Netherlands in the 1960s. Before the oil price crash late in 2008, Russia's natural resource windfall over the preceding years was a leading example). The illness may flare up with contemporary efforts to scale up foreign aid to achieve the Millennium Development Goals.

## Foreign Capital Flows

The instability of international (primarily financial) capital movements adds to the complications. Financial capital can take the form of both short- and long-term loans from abroad and, more recently, portfolio investments used to acquire domestic assets such as real estate and equity. Local booms in "asset prices" (equity, real estate, and foreign holdings) can be generated by but can also induce such capital flows. National balance sheets develop "maturity mismatches" (the loans are short-term but are being used to acquire long-term assets) and "currency mismatches" (loans are in hard currency, but local assets are valued in local currency). As with the Dutch disease, the local currency tends to get stronger. Chapter 7 goes into detail about linkages between capital flows and the exchange rate.

Internal financial flows can mimic these stock imbalances (Foley 2003). A boom in investment (in real estate, for example) can outrun increases in profits. Firms are forced in the direction of borrowing to cover shortfalls in retained earnings as interest rates may be going up. In Minsky's (1975) evocative terminology, financial flow positions shift from being "hedged" or rationally "speculative" toward an unstable "Ponzi" situation.[12]

Evidently the stage is being set for a crash—new money will not keep arriving in increasing quantities forever. After a time, speculation against the financial mismatches and the strong exchange rate mounts, and a run follows. There were famous crises in Latin America's "Southern Cone" (Argentina, Chile, and Uruguay) around 1980, and they continued through Mexico in 1994 and East Asia and Russia in the late 1990s, not to mention many other less publicized cases.[13] Episodes in Central and Eastern Europe in late 2008 are more recent examples.

This recurring cycle is fed by changing perceptions about "emerging markets" by investors. Alternating bursts of "appetite for risk" (with developing country assets usually viewed as "risky") and "flight to quality" (reduction in risky investments and increased demand for assets viewed as "safe," particularly treasury bonds of industrial countries) are common in financial markets as opinions shift along lines discussed by Keynes (1936) in his famous "beauty contest."[14] When emerging markets are in vogue, money pours in and interest rate "spreads"[15] on borrowing narrow; the reverse happens when there is capital flight. Such volatility is exacerbated by "contagion," meaning that groups of developing countries are pooled into risk categories in which probable financial returns are perceived (with or without empirical justification) to be strongly correlated.

Exchange rate spreads also complicate monetary policy. If controls over capital movements are absent or weak, the domestic interest rate will tend to equalize with the foreign rate + the spread + expected exchange rate depreciation. This "parity" rate will exacerbate the cycle, falling in an upswing as capital inflows come in large quantities, and rising in the crisis when capital flows out, in both cases frustrating efforts at counter-cyclical monetary interventions.[16]

## Macroeconomic Policy Space

Under the Washington consensus, macro policy design centered on reducing inflation or external deficits, leaving aside the old focus of Keynesian policies on full employment and of development policies on investment and growth. "Inflation targeting" as a rationale for interest rate management by central banks is the most recent incantation with regard to the first objective, while a "twin deficit" view of external balance continues to dominate orthodox discourse about the balance of payments.[17] Both lines of argument stress the need for fiscal and monetary austerity. But that can easily run counter to a developmental agenda.

As previously argued, development goals are easier to reach under a favorable configuration of macroeconomic prices, specifically a low and stable real interest rate and a weak and stable real exchange rate. In relation to the level of activity, a stable fiscal position with a deficit (or surplus) consistent with the economy's overall resource balance is also desirable.[18]

Nonetheless, a cyclically stable fiscal position and a favorable macro price constellation are difficult to put into place, let alone maintain. The maintenance problem arises because both private (domestic and foreign) and government economic behavior in developing countries is often pro-cyclical.

A basic reason, as we have already pointed out, is the instability of external financing. Thus, during upswings the private sector or government may increase its spending more rapidly than income—precisely because financing is available. Aggregate demand will go up, feeding back into further output expansion and debt accumulation—evidently an unsustainable situation. When external financing is cut, aggregate demand will tend to decrease more rapidly than income, feeding the downswing.

Fiscal policy has traditionally been used for counter-cyclical purposes in rich countries. In the developing world, the practice can be more difficult. The authorities in an impoverished society cannot easily refuse to spend extra revenues during an upswing. Fiscal restraint is even harder if local authorities were pressed by their lenders to adopt austerity programs during the preceding crisis to generate "credibility" in financial markets. A consequence is that in a subsequent upswing, the authorities face strong political pressure to spend and are only too happy to have breathing space to pursue expansionary policies.

In relation to monetary and exchange rate policies, the authorities are often thought to confront a "trilemma" stating that central bank interventions cannot simultaneously combine (1) full capital mobility, (2) a controlled exchange rate, and (3) independent monetary policy. Supposedly, only two of these policy lines can be consistently maintained.

The trilemma as just stated is a textbook theorem that is, in fact, invalid.[19] Even with free capital mobility, a central bank can in principle undertake transactions in both foreign exchange and domestic bond markets (not to mention other monetary control maneuvers) targeting both the interest and the exchange rates (Taylor 2004; Frenkel 2007).

Nevertheless, something like a trilemma can exist in the eyes of financial markets. There are practical limits to the volume of interventions that a central bank can practice, along with complicated feedbacks. In particular, central bank interventions to sterilize capital inflows or outflows may change interest rate expectations, whereas interventions in foreign exchange markets affect exchange rate expectations. These feedbacks may run counter to the objectives of monetary and foreign exchange policy.

Overcoming the trilemma and running a truly independent monetary and foreign exchange policy are simpler when there is an excess supply of foreign exchange. When foreign exchange is constraining economic policy and economic activity, international reserves previously accumulated by the central bank also provide some policy space to overcome the trilemma, but such space is more limited, as it depends on external financing being available.

The implication is that if it wishes to target the real exchange and interest rates, the central bank has to maintain tolerable control over the macroeconomic impacts of cross-border financial flows. As described in chapter 7, measures are available for this task. They do not work perfectly but can certainly moderate inflows during a boom and help to avoid an otherwise inevitable crash.[20]

If capital outflows are too large to manage with normal exchange rate and monetary policies, the authorities certainly do not want to engage in recession-triggering monetary contraction. If the exchange rate has been maintained at a relatively depreciated level, the external deficit is not setting off financial alarm bells, and inflation is under control, then there are no "fundamental" reasons for market participants to expect a maxi-devaluation. Under such circumstances, the way for the authorities to maintain a policy regime consistent with targeted macro prices is to impose exchange controls and restrictions on capital outflows.

## Institutions and the State

The development and macroeconomic policies on which we focus in this book[21] have to be developed within a given "institutional" framework of laws, political processes, and the general sociocultural environment.[22] We should start by pointing out that in economic analysis the word "institutions" is used in at least two senses—as "rules of the game" and "organizations." Examples are property rights, on the one hand, and a central bank, on the other. Rules may be formalized as in law or be informal.[23] They may or may not support growth and structural change. Similarly, the form of an institution such as an "independent" central bank may or may not lead it to function in a desirable way.

We don't directly take on the question of how institutions evolve, but in principle they can either be imported from abroad (subject to indigenous modification), as in Japan after its "opening" by Commodore Perry in 1854, or emerge largely subject to domestic forces. Context is of fundamental importance. "Mercantilist" institutions arose in nations seeking to escape the thralls of comparative advantage in producing raw materials. For Marx and Friedrich Engels, technical change drove the transformation of feudalism into a mode of production (a cultural-institutional-technological complex) centered on the bourgeoisie. In macroeconomics, introducing the institution of wage and price indexation to ongoing inflation can lead to explosive price increases later on (an example of an institution with apparently desirable short-run effects on income distribution but having unforeseen, undesirable long-term repercussions).

At any point in time, an economy will operate within an institutional complex having a degree of stability—after all, institutions are supposed to persist, at least for some duration. But to paraphrase Marx, people change institutions although not in an institutional environment of their own choosing. Policy makers can attempt to facilitate useful changes, but institutions themselves make up an important component of the structural limitations within which they must maneuver.

## Institutions

Thinking about institutions as factors that must be understood as fencing in available policy choices in differing national contexts diverges sharply from much recent academic literature in development economics, e.g., Acemoglu and Robinson (2005) in *Economic Origins of Dictatorship and Democracy* (a title drawn from that of the classic book by the historical sociologist Barrington Moore Jr., whose own ideas about evolving institutions are discussed later in this chapter). They and other authors focus on the rule of law and efficient private property rights as set forth by North (1990), which are supposed to cut back on "transactions costs" associated with economic activity. Getting rid of corruption and improving quality of "governance" are other favored metrics for a country's ability to undertake growth-promoting policy changes.

This diagnosis is rooted in an old idea in economics—that "agents" simply maximize their utility or profits subject to a given set of constraints. Causality clearly runs from culture (Confucianism, the Protestant ethic, etc.), natural endowments—and who controls them, technology, and existing institutions to economic development. That agents themselves may have "agency" in the modification of institutions and that development itself can stimulate institutional and technological change does not always enter the picture. As previously noted, this evolutionary process takes place within an existing historical context. Attempts on the part of international donor and financial organizations to introduce alien (usually ersatz Anglo-Saxon) institutions "as recommended by economic theory" can very easily backfire.

A key version of the mainstream view—originating before Adam Smith, first clearly stated by the "Austrian" school from Vienna in the 1870s, and trumpeted for developing countries in extreme form by de Soto (2000)—asserts that rapid growth can only emerge from private entrepreneurship under clear property rights protection. Austrian economists do not recognize the state as a potential entrepreneur or as a supporter of entrepreneurship.

In less strident versions, the Austrian argument dominates much current discussion of aid and development policy, especially among major donors. The Washington consensus, now in remission, strongly emphasized private sector initiatives and strict limits on state guidance of the economy. Over the past two or three decades many foreign aid and development policy packages informed by the consensus did not generate linkages among demand growth, productivity, and employment. In a classic example of "blame the victim," mainstream economics has recently been hinting that poor institutions and governance are the reasons its own policies over the past two or three decades have not succeeded in stimulating growth. To put the reasoning childishly: "We gave you good policies, they didn't work, so it's your fault because of your terrible institutions."

## Theories of Capitalism

This discussion brings us to the broader debate on the role of the state in a market-oriented economy. In this debate, there is a fundamental confusion between theories of capitalism, on the one hand, and analysis of what the state can do and does, on the other. In the *Communist Manifesto*, for example, Marx and Engels tell us that "the executive of the modern state is but a committee for managing the common affairs of the whole bourgeoisie." This statement may or may not be correct but says nothing about how the executive committee handles its day-to-day operations or even what they are.

At the other end of the political spectrum, the Coase (1960) "theorem" (really an informal statement of principle) claims that, in the absence of transaction costs, all government allocations of property rights are equally efficient, because interested parties will bargain privately to correct any externality. Adherents further believe that transactions are in fact inexpensive or else think that the state should devote all its efforts to driving the costs down. Coase's ideas strongly influenced North and followers in their emphasis on property rights as the basic institutional foundation of modern capitalism.

Somewhere in the middle, the World Bank at various times has asserted, following dominant institutional analysis as applied to development and previously outlined, that "market friendliness," is the skeleton key to successful economic development. That recommendation is not far from saying that the state should just act to make transactions easier, in effect putting the bank closer to Coase's view.

Neither Marx nor Coase marks the end of the day in the discussion of capitalism. There are many theories that most economists have never encountered, let alone contemplated in a serious way. To have a sensible discussion of the state in a capitalist economy, it is essential to ask what a capitalist economy is. In so doing, we necessarily enter into an "overdetermined" situation, with too many explanations for a single reality.[24] Thus all we can do in this discussion is to sketch a few approaches to capitalism that may be of use in dealing with practical policy issues.

Marx and Engels are presumably well enough known not to need discussion. For present purposes, their emphasis on relatively well-defined social groups and on how they limit possibilities for economic change is precisely to the point. Capitalism becomes a system of institutionalized strife among the competing groups (Collins 1980).

This way of looking at the world resonates with a large school of socioeconomic historians. The doyen, Karl Polanyi (1944), emphasized that the state is the central economic actor: "The road to the free market [in Western Europe] was opened and kept open by an enormous increase in continuous, centrally organized and controlled interventionism" (p. 140). In Polanyi's view, the institutions that support capitalism arise from within the society that also defends itself against the worst excesses such as slavery and child labor. A "double movement" of creating and then regulating market institutions occurs system-wide, with the state as the superordinate actor.

States, of course, can fail—in many dimensions. They operate under fundamental uncertainty and may or may not respond to uneven advances in different sectors, disproportionalities, and balance of payments and inflationary pressures, as well as the social tensions that inevitably arise in the development process (Hirschman 1958). They can try to do too much, achieving little. They can become purely predatory, as in countless petty dictatorships around the world. But when backward economies do catch up, the process is mediated by the state, in particular on the basis of administrative guidance practiced by an autonomous bureaucracy accepted by (and embedded in) the society overall.

Power relationships among collective actors are central to the strife. Barrington Moore (1966) pursues a comparative-historical analysis of how interactions among lords and peasants, bourgeoisie and the state gave rise to nineteenth- and twentieth-century economic and political structures (bourgeois revolutionary, capitalist reactionary, and communist, in his classification) that constrain economic policy.

Moore has many counterpart sociological historians. Tilly (1992), for example, sets up a model involving the degree of coercion imposed by the state and the stock of capital. As in any model, there are oversimplifications. He emphasizes two: metonymy, through which the actions of the "ruler" summarize all the activities of the state; and reification, meaning that all groups of actors have unitary interests.

From this perspective, there can be an equilibrium between the degree of coercion and the capital stock. There is a long-term reduction in the power to coerce as accumulation proceeds, and there are also decreasing returns to coercion itself. There are many possible outcomes: a "capital-intensive" trajectory, a "coercion-intensive" path, and a "capitalized coercion" path in between.

In the history of the European state system, Russia and Poland were coercion-intensive while the Italian city-states and the Netherlands concentrated on accumulation. The large Western European countries—Britain, France, Spain, and Prussia—practiced capitalized coercion. The Nordics were initially coercive but veered toward capitalized coercion in the eighteenth century. In line with Gerschenkron's (1962) emphasis on how relative "backwardness" conditions the possibilities for economic development, there was an implicit division of control of the economy between the state and private actors along all these paths. As discussed later in this chapter, there is always a tension in policy formation between the clumsy thumb of the state with its powers of coercion and the nimble fingers of capitalists who can deal with their own concerns but lack power and ignore or, at least, do not fully internalize the need to improve social relationships more generally.

Continuing with the theme of overdetermination, there is a long tradition of seeing the birth of capitalism as the result of certain mental attitudes, with Adam Smith's "propensity to truck and barter" being an important early entry in the list. Another famous example is Max Weber's invocation of the Protestant ethic, which he said meant that a believer felt the need to *prove* (not earn) his right to eternal salvation through methodical labor and restrained consumption. The entrepreneurial spirit emphasized by the Austrian school is another variation on that theme. There is also the confusing discussion on Confucianism in East Asia. Weber thought that this belief system held back China's development while recently it has been touted as a major factor underlying the growth of the Tigers.

The French Annales school of historians, with their emphasis on the *histoire des mentalités*, represents the peak of this line of analysis. Fernand Braudel's (1979) fascinating three volumes on *Capitalism and Material Life* go into minute detail on how people made economies work. Braudel mixes more or less standard economics material with much description of the social impact of economic events on everyday life and pays great attention to food, fashion, social customs, and many other themes. Slaves, serfs, and peasants play the major roles in his history, not capitalists and kings.

In yet another line of history, individual actors are overwhelmed by disease, geography, or the environment. On the coercion side of the equation, in an important book, McNeill (1976) points out that disease resistance won and lost wars (recall the effect of smallpox in permitting the conquest of Mexico by Cortes). Populations expanded when they had dealt with epidemic disease either by learning how to prevent it or developing immunity. Epidemics profoundly shaped subsequent economic history, as with the plague in Europe.

The idea that geography and the environment interact in determining economic destiny dates to antiquity (the Greek geographer Strabo wrote that climate influences the psychological disposition of different races) and has cropped up many times since. The latest blockbuster is Jared Diamond's (1999) *Guns, Germs, and Steel*, which makes a strong ecologically based argument for the dominance of Eurasian societies in the world. They pioneered domestication and the use of food grains and therefore reaped the benefits. The unstated message is that sustained economic growth may not be in the cards for the geographically disenfranchised regions of the world—much of Africa, the Americas, and Austronesia. Most economists would beg to differ, but could they be wrong?

Against this bright and varied firmament of ideas, current mainstream economists' views of the factors underlying capitalism do not shine very strongly. Property rights are no doubt an important aspect of capitalist development, but attempting to make them into the central institutional factor is idle if not entirely misplaced.

## What the State Can Do

Suppose that the overdetermined socioeconomic system throws up some sort of market economy in a country with a state that has some power of coercion, or "authority," in the usage of Charles Lindblom (1977) in his classic book on *Politics and Markets*. How can it use the authority to guide the economy successfully?

An initial point, already mentioned, is that coercion or authority is all thumbs, perhaps strong ones, but thumbs nevertheless. The state is not as good as the market in terms of economic initiative and resourcefulness. As a consequence, in growing economies the state delegates some of its authority over the economy to market actors. Perhaps with difficulty, the state always has the power to take it back.[25]

Market actors, on the other hand, can sustain economic growth if adequately directed and restrained from mere cupidity. But there are associated costs. Standard property rights make capitalists the owners of enterprises, with vast consequences for the distribution of wealth and political power, access to the government, control of the media, job rights, alienation, and social conflict. But if adult noncapitalists can use their own property rights to hold money or physical assets, then they can (to an extent) pay capitalists to use nimble fingers to produce goods and services to satisfy their needs. The market can fulfill this function more effectively than the state. But it cannot deliver many public goods on its own, in which case compulsion, coercion, or guidance may be required.

In practice, then, there are two sets of authorities—government officials and businesspeople. They share an interest in system stability, which in a poor country necessarily requires economic growth per capita. The issue at hand is how growth can be attained. About the only tools available involve cooperation and mutually reinforcing feedback between the two groups of actors, best with a voice for peasants, workers, and households as well. The ways the tools can be used will differ across time and space, but the examples previously presented in this chapter and discussed in the chapters that follow show that they can be effective.

## Notes

1. At times we refer to developing and transition economies separately but generally use the terms "developing" countries or economies and "developing world" to refer to both groups.
2. In simple terms, think of the value of bread a baker sells over a year minus costs of inputs for its production (flour, water, electricity, etc.).
3. Again, in simple terms, a "real" economic magnitude means a value (sales of bread, for example) divided by a price (price of bread).
4. The Ramsey and Solow models differ mainly in their hypotheses regarding factors explaining the level of savings.
5. One joule is the energy required to lift a small (100 gram) apple one meter against the earth's gravity. One terajoule is roughly equivalent to 7,700 gallons of gasoline or 31 tons of coal. Thinking in terms of power, one watt equals one joule of energy use per second. Dividing by the number of seconds in a year shows that an American worker utilizes 19.3 kilowatts of power to produce his or her contribution to real GDP. An African uses 300 watts.
6. For further details on the estimates of energy/labor ratios for developed and developing countries, see Taylor (2008a).
7. A third asymmetry is that labor, particularly unskilled labor, is much less mobile internationally than capital, but this fact is less relevant for the analysis in this book.

8. The Kaldor and Rada models are discussed in more detail in chapter 8. A nonformalized version of these models was presented in Ocampo and Taylor (1998) and Ocampo
(2005).

9. The term "Robber Barons" in the United States originated in the second half of the
nineteenth century. The idea is that "business leaders in the United States from about
1865 to 1900 were, on the whole, a set of avaricious rascals who habitually cheated and
robbed investors and consumers, corrupted government, fought ruthlessly among
themselves, and in general carried on predatory activities comparable to those of the
robber barons of medieval Europe" (Hal 1958).

10. We express the exchange rate in standard fashion as units of home currency (pesos or
rupees, for example) per one unit of foreign currency (dollar or euro). When it is calculated in this fashion, an appreciated or stronger exchange rate has a *lower* value.

11. As previously discussed, when foreign net borrowing is negative, the country actually
becomes a net *lender* to other countries (curiously enough, many times to industrial
countries, as indeed has been the most common pattern in recent years).

12. In a bit more detail, a flow position is "hedged" when investment is less than gross profits
and "speculative" when investment exceeds profits net of interest payments. With high
investment, "Ponzi" finance comes in when profits fail to cover interest payments.

13. Writing in draft form before the Southern Cone events, Roberto Frenkel (1983) pre-
sciently pointed out how they could come to pass.

14. Keynes contest was not to pick the most beautiful person (or asset) but rather to guess
the person that average opinion will choose as the winner.

15. Spreads are the premiums that countries must pay over international interest rates
that are used as a reference for "safe" assets, particularly U.S. Treasury bonds.

16. The significance of parity rates was perhaps first pointed out Keynes (1923).

17. See chapter 7 for more on inflation targeting and the theory of twin deficits. The latter
says that reducing the fiscal deficit should lead to an improved external position. The
data presented in chapter 5 support no such linkage.

18. As previously noted, a convenient way to analyze resource balances is in terms of flows
of net borrowing (=investment – saving=income – expenditure) of the public, foreign,
and private sectors. Also, an important accounting rule is that net-borrowing flows
economy-wide must sum to zero. Its implications are developed in chapters 5 and 7.

19. Appendix 7.1 goes into more detail on the failure of the trilemma and models of exchange rate determination more generally.

20. This danger also exists in poor countries if a "boom" in aid inflows were to be sud-
denly cut off—by no means a geopolitical impossibility. The familiar Dutch disease
analysis of adverse effects of foreign aid applies to this situation.

21. Some attention is also paid to more humanly oriented educational, health, social protection, and distributive activities, although we do not address questions of how to
extend "entitlements" or "freedoms" to individuals as emphasized by Sen (2000), in
part because their feedback effects on growth appear to be rather weak.

22. The following discussion draws on papers collected in Chang (2007).

23. Local, often tacit agreements governing exploitation of common property resources
are important examples of the latter. Property rights in contemporary China (including those for town-and-village enterprises) are a complicated mixture of formal and
informal rules and regulations, with a good dose of politics thrown in.

24. The idea goes back to Sigmund Freud, who thought that the content of dreams was
shaped by factors ranging from recent events in the dreamer's life ("the residue of the
day") to repressed traumas and unconscious wishes. It has been influential in fields
ranging from literary criticism to Marxist political theory.

25. Central banks are an interesting example of the state and private sector interrelationship. An "independent" central bank is a quasi-market actor because it can set interest rates on its own, in principle without consulting the rest of the government (though of course it is subject to political pressure). But historically central banks were created to manage activities previously exercised by the private sector, e.g., the U.S. Federal Reserve took over the role of lender of last resort played by the banker J. Pierpont Morgan in a series of financial crises around the turn of the twentieth century.

CHAPTER 2

# Growth and Policy Space in Historical Terms

## (WITH MARIÁNGELA PARRA)

I N THIS CHAPTER, we take up the history of income growth in developing economies and the changes in the international environment in which they operate. Details about structural change in several dimensions are presented in the following two chapters.

### Trends in Real Income Levels per Capita

Observation of regional growth experiences in now rich and poor countries since the early nineteenth century clearly shows that there has been no overall convergence of per capita incomes. Instead, the income gap widened considerably in both relative and absolute terms. The growth rates of GDP per capita for the countries that were most advanced in 1820 were the highest throughout the nineteenth and twentieth centuries. According to Maddison (1995, 2001, 2007), in the "purchasing power parity" (PPP) terms that have become commonplace in making such comparisons, by 1992 Western Europe had a 13-fold increase in GDP per capita over its level in 1820. The Western Offshoots (United States, Canada, Australia, and New Zealand) enjoyed a 17-fold increase, while Latin America and Asia respectively increased seven and six times compared to 1820. Figure 2.1 shows ratios of PPP per capita incomes in Maddison's developing country regions to per capita income in the "old" OECD (Organization for Economic Co-operation and Development)—consisting of Western Europe and Western Offshoots but not Japan for reference years during 1820–2003.[1]

The generally negative slopes of the curves are disheartening. Over this long period, PPP per capita income ratios for Latin America and Eastern Europe fell by more than 50 percent, and the proportional loss for Africa was even greater. Toward the end of the twentieth century, the ratios for China and India

**FIGURE 2.1**

## Ratios of GDP per capita (developing countries/"old" OECD countries [1820–2003])

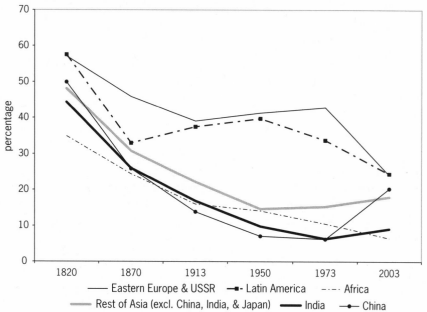

—— Eastern Europe & USSR   —■- Latin America   – - – Africa
━━━ Rest of Asia (excl. China, India, & Japan)   ━━ India   —●— China
*Source*: GDP and population levels from Maddison (2007).

began to go up from levels of less than 0.1 observed five decades earlier and which had continued to fall even during the third quarter of the century, the era of rapid growth worldwide generally referred to as the "golden age." The "rest of Asia," which includes about 12.5 percent of Asia's population without Japan, China, and India (with Indonesia as the most populous country followed by South Korea), moved gradually up since the mid-twentieth century, most remarkably in the case of the Tigers.

Figure 2.2 shows PPP ratios for selected regions in the second half of the twentieth century (the rich countries now include Japan).[2] The Tigers are the only group showing a sustained increase over most of the period, accelerating in the last quarter of the century to reach 70 percent of the level of income in the developed economies. There was modest catching-up on the part of the rest of the Asian regions in the last 25 years, and a remarkable one in the case of China.

During the "golden age," the ratios for the other regions remained roughly constant with two major exceptions, sub-Saharan Africa and Latin America.

FIGURE 2.2

## Catching up: GDP per capita of developing countries compared with OECD countries (1950–2006)

(A)  South Asia, East Asia, China, and Tigers

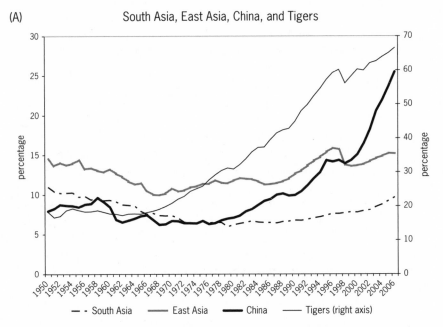

- · South Asia    East Asia    China    Tigers (right axis)

(B)  Africa, Middle East, Latin America, Former USSR, and Eastern Europe

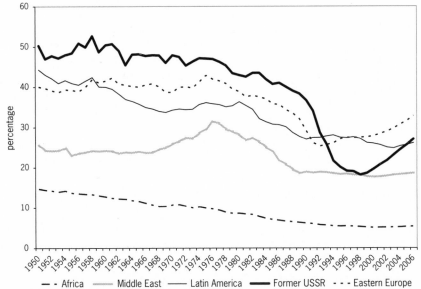

- · Africa    Middle East    Latin America    Former USSR   - - - Eastern Europe

*Sources*: GDP and population levels from Maddison (2007). GDP and population levels for 2003–2006 from World Bank (2007).

However, Latin America had been the success story of the developing world from 1870 to 1950, so in 1973 the ratio of its income relative to that of industrial countries was still above that of the Tigers. The regional average during the third quarter of the twentieth century includes poor performances of some countries (notably Argentina) combined with very good performance of others (notably Brazil and Mexico). The Middle East was obviously a success story during the oil boom of the 1970s.

Later, and particularly in the last two decades of the twentieth century, income in all of these other regions declined, most notably for the Middle East and the formerly socialist countries that were parts of the Soviet Union. Central and Eastern Europe also experienced a decline during its transition to capitalism, but started to recover much earlier than the former members of the USSR. Even several successful Asian economies fell back for a while as a result of the 1997 Asian financial crisis.

This "great divergence" of the last quarter of the twentieth century is especially disturbing because the decline in the income ratios in several instances was attributable to stagnation or a decrease in the absolute value of GDP per capita of the follower countries. For example, by 1998, Africa's GDP per capita had decreased 14 percent with respect to the already low 1977 levels.[3] The Middle East is another region with an absolute fall in income per capita at the end of the century—10 percent between 1977 and 1998. Lastly, the former USSR lost ground in record time, with its per capita income collapsing by an astonishing 45 percent from 1989 to 1998—a story that characterized in variable degrees most former socialist countries in Central and Eastern Europe during the first years of transition.

More recently, and until the collapse that took place since the third quarter of 2008, the rise in export prices of raw materials, oil, and other basic commodities, mixed with favorable developments in international financial markets, helped the developing world recover some of the relative income lost since the mid-1970s. By 2003 (the last year for which the Maddison series are estimated), this trend was noticeable in most regions, with the major exceptions being Latin America and, to a lesser extent, Africa.[4] The recovery from the Asian financial crisis was not uniform and was clearly weaker in the rest of East Asia than in the Tigers.

However, although *all* developing country groups managed to grow faster than industrial countries during 2003–2007, which is an unprecedented historical development, all income ratios were still significantly lower at the end of this boom than in 1950, except for the East Asian regions (Tigers, East Asia, and China), So, as this book went to press, the story for most of the developing world continued to be that of "Divergence, Big Time," to use Pritchett's (1997) terminology.

# Fluctuations in Growth

Another way of looking at this history is in terms of growth rates as opposed to levels. In the second half of the twentieth century, there was a pattern of growth successes and collapses at the country level. Numerical evidence is summarized in table 2.1. Between two-fifths and one-half of developing countries experienced a decent rate of growth per capita (25 percent per decade or a bit over 2 percent per year) from the 1950s to the 1970s; this proportion fell to less than one-fifth during the lost decade of the 1980s. At the same time, the number of countries experiencing growth collapses increased sharply, reaching a peak during the lost decade, when about one-half of developing countries suffered a reduction in per capita GDP. A full one-third of them went through a severe growth collapse (fall in GDP per capita of over 10 percent in the decade).

As already discussed in this chapter, the situation reversed modestly during the 1990s when roughly a third of the developing countries managed to grow at more than 2 percent annually, and the proportion of severe growth collapses fell to about one-fifth of the countries. During the early twenty-first -century boom, the proportion of developing countries experiencing rapid growth reached levels comparable to those of the golden age, with about 64 percent growing at least at a rate of 2 percent per capita per year. However, negative growth experiences remained more frequent than before.

Overall, growth successes and collapses tended to cluster in specific time periods. The outstanding difference between the golden age or the recent boom and the great divergence of the late twentieth century is the significant increase

**TABLE 2.1**

**Developing Countries' Successes and Collapses: Percentage of Total Number of Countries Categorized by Cumulative Growth Rate of GDP per Capita**

|  |  | 1950–1960 | 1960–1970 | 1970–1980 | 1980–1990 | 1990–2000 | 2000–2006 |
|---|---|---|---|---|---|---|---|
| Cumulative growth | >25% | 44 | 51 | 46 | 18 | 34 | 46 |
|  | >50% | 12 | 19 | 2 | 1 | 1 | 18 |
|  | <0% | 6 | 8 | 25 | 53 | 31 | 12 |
|  | <−10% | 2 | 3 | 17 | 33 | 21 | 3 |

*Sources:* 118 countries for 1950–2000 based on Maddison (2007; 1990 Geary-Khamis dollars, PPP), 112 countries for 2000–2006 based on World Development Indicators (World Bank 2007; constant 2005 international $, PPP).

*Note:* For the last period, the indicators on cumulative growth are based on the average annual growth rates for 2000–2006, which if maintained over a decade are equivalent to the specified decade growth rates.

FIGURE 2.3

## The global development cycle (1951–2006)

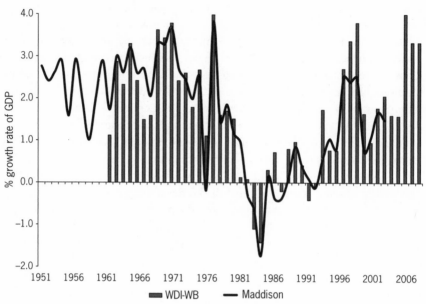

Sources: Ocampo and Parra (2007), based on data from Maddison (2007) and World Bank (2007).

in the frequency of growth collapses and the much lower frequency of sustainable growth successes over the 1980s and 1990s.[5]

The clustering in time of successes and failures can also be seen in figure 2.3. Abstracting from the previously noted regional differences, rapid growth from the 1950s through the early 1970s was followed by a strong downward trend[6] in average developing country growth since the late 1970s, which reached its lowest point in the early 1980s. Average growth continued to be low until the early 1990s but then was followed by a recovery, which was nonetheless interrupted for several years by the Asian and Russian crises of 1997 and 1998.

It is unlikely that domestic reasons alone can explain such a clustering in time of booms and growth collapses. Common external factors must have played a significant role, some with strong regional dimensions. It is not surprising that the end of the golden age of the industrial world also marked (with a lag) the end of the golden age of development. But the average performance of developing countries since then follows a different dynamic from that of industrial countries, reflecting the specific effects of the changing international environment.

## Changes in the International Environment

As discussed in chapter 1, the end of the golden age also coincided with a major shift in the orientation of development policy. The transition was traumatic in several parts of the developing world, as the evidence from the previous section indicates.

Besides the change in policy, two major and largely unexpected shocks hit in the late 1970s. They were the interest rate shock of 1979, illustrated in figure 2.4, which was triggered by stagflation (slow growth combined with rising inflation) during the 1970s in advanced economies and a structural downward shift of the terms of trade of commodities (see figure 4.3 in chapter 4).

The worldwide interest rate shock had no historical precedents. After explicit policy decisions were imposed (notably by the U.S. Federal Reserve Bank), inflation in the rich countries promptly receded but real interest rates stayed high. Using the 10-year U.S. Treasury note as a benchmark, the real rate increased from –1.8 percent per year in 1979 to 3.6 percent in 1981, reaching a peak of 8.2 percent in 1984. The rate increase faced by developing countries was far

FIGURE 2.4

**Percentage of developing countries with debt/GNI ratios above 50% and 100% respectively, and the 10-year U.S. treasury notes real interest rate**

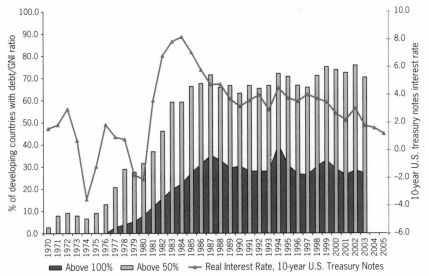

*Sources*: Ocampo and Parra (2007), based on World Bank (2006).

UN/DPAD stands for United Nations/Development Policy and Analysis Division.

higher, from 2.5 percent in 1979 to 22 percent in 1981 in real terms, as the average risk premia added to LIBOR (London Interbank Offered Rate) that they paid simultaneously rose.[7] After having benefited from the recycling of petro-dollars, developing countries suffered a substantial shock that implied, for many of them, significant balance of payments distress.

The non-oil commodity terms-of-trade shock did have precedents, but only in the distant past (in the 1920s). Real non-oil commodity prices went through a structural downward shift of over 30 percent, breaking the long stretch since the 1920s when they had been essentially trendless (Ocampo and Parra 2003). The price index of manufactures exported by developing countries, relative to manufactures exported by developed countries, experienced a simultaneous downturn (Akyüz 2003, chap. 2).

The unprecedented character of the interest rate shock and the distant memory of a comparable terms-of-trade shock explain the unexpectedly large magnitude of ex-post risks that the developing world had to confront.

Debt dynamics turned explosive after the interest rate shock, with both short- and long-term effects. The proportion of developing countries with moderate debt ratios (over 50 percent of GNI) had been rising from the mid-1970s but was still low prior to the shock, whereas the proportion with critical debt ratios (over 100 percent of GNI) was very low (figure 2.4). Both increased sharply and remained at high levels for the next quarter century, for three basic reasons.

The first is that real interest rates remained high: over 4.5 percent for almost twenty years for the 10-year U.S. Treasury rate. They only returned to low real levels in the early 2000s.

The second reason was a lack of international institutions to manage debt overhangs, in sharp contrast to the 1930s when one such "institution" was available: broad-based moratoria. A few means to deal with overhangs emerged, but had only weak effects: the Brady plan of the late 1980s and the Heavily Indebted Poor Countries (HIPC) initiative of the mid-1990s, followed by the Multilateral Debt Relief (MDR) initiative launched after the Gleneagles meeting of the G8 economies in 2005.

The third reason was that, alongside the hike in interest rates, net financial flows to developing economies became negative, indeed highly negative until the early 1990s for many of them. The early 1990s saw a recovery in such flows, but the succession of the Asian and Russian crises of the late 1990s and their contagion effects on other developing countries interrupted this recovery. These events had, nonetheless, weaker and more temporary repercussions than the debt crisis of the 1980s.

After 2003, capital flows to developing countries began again to boom. This factor, together with low real interest rates and the HIPC/MDR initiatives finally broke the long-term debt overhangs of many developing countries. At the same time, commodity prices boomed from 2004 until the first half of 2008 (see figure 4.3 in chapter 4). Therefore, the two shocks that generated the "lost decade" waned or lost strength, leading to the 2003–2007 developing country recovery. However, favorable financial conditions weakened since the outbreak of the U.S. financial crises in mid-2007 and came to a halt with the global financial meltdown of September 2008. In turn, the commodity price boom weakened after mid-2008 and was followed by a free price fall during the financial meltdown.

The favorable trends that took place in 2003–2007 are part of a broader set that reflects striking changes that have occurred in the global economy. One important factor is the growing weight of China and, to a lesser extent, of India and other East Asian economies, which contributed until 2008 to the overall demand for raw materials exported by other developing countries.

Financial flows and Chinese investment in the developing world were also substantial. A set of third-world multinational enterprises took off, investing in other developing countries, and even in the industrial world. Countries with surpluses in their balance of payments (primarily oil-exporting countries and high savers in East Asia) created or capitalized sovereign wealth funds, and a larger group of developing countries accumulated large amounts of foreign exchange reserves.

These developments led to the expectation that economic downturn and financial events taking place in the United States and Europe since mid-2007 could be counteracted by self-propelling growth in the developing world. In this view, the economic rise of China, India, and the East Asian countries could for the first time allow the developing world to "decouple" from adverse trends in the industrial world, by acting as an autonomous engine of growth and as a significant source of finance.

However, as this book went to press, it was already evident that the developing countries had been strongly hit by the world financial crisis and that the decoupling story had been no more than a dream. Many developing countries may, nonetheless, manage to avoid recession, and in this sense they would continue to "converge" toward the income of industrial countries. However, for the immediate future, this continued convergence will be a reflection of regression in the industrial world, not of a broad-based dynamic growth experienced by developing countries.

On a more positive note, to the extent that official development assistance to the poorest countries of the world continues to increase, based on the commitments made in recent years (and only partly realized as of 2008), it would help the poorest countries of the world maintain part of their growth momentum. The following section describes an important example—the effects that commodity prices, foreign aid, and other factors have had on economic performance in parts of sub-Saharan Africa over the current decade.

## Sub-Saharan Africa During the Current Decade

At the continent-wide level, growth post-2000 until 2007–2008 in SSA was largely an oil-driven phenomenon.[8] Merchandise exports from three major oil exporters (Nigeria, Equatorial Guinea, and Angola) increased from $30 billion in 2000 to $114.7 billion in 2007, or roughly a 21 percent compound rate over the seven-year period. Oil made up the bulk of merchandise export dynamism for SSA as a whole, as the three countries' exports rose from 47.4 to 59.8 percent of the regional total (excluding South Africa's). Both price and quantity changes contributed to this outcome. The average barter terms of trade for the three countries increased by 78 percent between 2000 and 2006.

In turn, growth rates of oil producers have all been above the average regional rate. Angola averaged GDP growth of 13.1 percent for 2001–2007, Equatorial Guinea 22.0 percent, and Nigeria 5.4 percent (6.7 percent in 2003–2007), Sudan 7.7 percent, Chad 10.9 percent, etc., compared to an average of 5.2 percent for all of SSA. Some non-oil producers showed more moderate growth increases in the last few years, again driven by recovery in the terms of trade. Zambia went from 3.3 percent growth in 2002 to a peak of 6.2 percent in 2006 when terms of trade increased by 100 percent attributable largely to the rise in copper prices.

There are some moderate growth improvements without a rise in the terms of trade. Kenya had stagnant terms of trade but used an export processing zone and AGOA (the United States' African Growth and Opportunity Act of 2000) access to increase textile exports to the United States, leading to a modest increase in the proportion of manufacturing exports from 21 to 26 percent in 2000–2004. However, such export growth through diversification is a rare exception in Africa with broad indexes of diversification falling in recent years. Nor have there been significant private capital inflows.

Although conflicting opinions remain on the table, aid-driven economic expansion also seems to have taken place in several cases. Minoiu and Reddy (2007) argue that aid can be effective in promoting growth in the long run if it is directed toward sectors such as infrastructure, education, or health. They suggest that harmonization of donors' intentions and the targeted use of aid for developmental goals is essential in determining aid effectiveness.

The recent positive shift in the industrialized world's commitment to provide official development assistance (ODA) to poor countries, especially in sub-Sahara Africa, emerged as a result of two UN-sponsored initiatives: the MDGs and the Monterrey Consensus. The *2008 Economic Report on Africa* (United Nations Economic Commission for Africa [UNECA] 2008) reports that, while net ODA flows to Africa have increased in the post-Monterrey period, from about $16 billion in 1998–2001 to $28 billion in recent years, progress on aid effectiveness[9]—promoting growth and development—lags in many cases. An exception is Mozambique, which has seen a significant improvement in its ability to disburse aid for developmental projects and consequently has seen solid growth in recent years. For other countries such as Kenya, Malawi, or Ghana, the relation between aid and economic growth has been undermined by the unpredictability of aid flows, bureaucratic bottlenecks on both donor's and recipient's sides, and overall misalignments between the conditions attached by donors and countries' developmental strategies. As discussed in chapter 7, much more work has to be done so that aid can promote dynamic economic growth and not just alleviate temporary economic hardship.

Economic changes and shocks related to trade or financial markets are not the only factors affecting economic performance in the region. The African continent overwhelmingly has led developing countries in terms of armed conflicts, especially during the 1980s and 1990s (Cramer 2002). In this area, advance has also been made, though significant conflicts remain in the continent. While we do not examine in this book the disruptive effects that wars and violence have had on economic activity or their causes, we acknowledge that they have worsened the weak economic performance and, particularly, the frequency of growth collapses in SSA in recent decades.

## Notes

1. For reasons discussed later in this chapter, relative income ratios of poor to rich countries are significantly lower when calculated in terms of market prices as opposed to PPP.
2. The regions broadly follow the configuration used by the *World Bank Development Indicators 2007* for Latin America and the Caribbean, Middle East, and North Africa, sub-Saharan Africa, and the high-income OECD countries. Eastern Europe in our analysis includes only Bulgaria, Czech Republic, Hungary, Poland, Romania, and Slovakia. The Tigers include South Korea, Malaysia, Singapore, and Taiwan, while East Asia comprises Myanmar, Cambodia, Indonesia, Laos, Mongolia, Philippines, Thailand, and Vietnam. Finally, South Asia includes Afghanistan, Bangladesh, India, Pakistan, Nepal, and Sri Lanka. The detailed analysis of sources of growth undertaken in chapter 3 will be based on slightly different configurations for the selected regions compared to the current chapter.
3. We refer to 1990 Geary-Khamis dollars, Maddison's preferred benchmark numéraire for computing PPP income levels.
4. We updated figure 2.2 to 2006 from Maddison's series using data from the World Bank (2007).
5. See a full analysis of this issue in Ocampo and Vos (2008, chap. 1).
6. Or there was a "cycle" or "oscillation," although whether or not the temporal pattern will recur as these words imply is an open question.
7. The LIBOR is an index of rates quoted by London banks. It serves as an international reference interest rate.
8. Thanks to Howard Stein for discussion of the issues considered in this section.

9. The Paris Declaration on Aid Effectiveness was adopted in 2005. It comprises several principles that attempt to enhance aid effectiveness, including ownership of the development strategies by recipient countries, harmonization of donor practices, and alignment of such practices with the recipient countries' strategies. Although some advance has been made, much remains to be done, and indeed significant disagreement remains about the precise meaning of these principles and the way to their implementation.

CHAPTER 3

# Growth Rates, Economic Structures, and Energy Use

THIS CHAPTER is about the growth and development performance of non-industrialized countries in the latter part of the twentieth century, in particular the "great divergence" of their growth rates of per capita GDP from those of the industrial world since around 1980 until the early part of the 2000s that was illustrated in chapter 2. The goal is to explore the factors underlying observed patterns of growth and trace out plausible lines of causation for their diversity. The analysis follows Kuznets (1966) in attempting to organize the data in such a way as to highlight salient relationships, or the lack thereof, among key economic variables.

To keep the discussion within bounds, the data are organized in terms of 12 regional groups including 57 developing and transition countries: rapidly growing East Asian economies (or the Tigers), Southeast Asia, China, South Asia, semi-industrialized countries (mostly from Latin America but also South Africa and Turkey with economic structures similar to their counterparts in the Western Hemisphere), the smaller Andean countries, Central America and the Caribbean, "representative" and "other" countries in sub-Saharan Africa,[1] the Middle East and Northern Africa, Central and Eastern Europe, and Russia and Ukraine representing the former USSR. The nations in each group are listed in appendix 3.1.

## Divergence in the Twentieth Century and Patterns of Output Growth

To set the discussion, figure 3.1 shows GDP and sectoral per capita output growth rates by region since 1970 in constant 1990 U.S. dollars.[2] We identify three cohorts of regions and countries that had similar patterns of growth:

In the first group, there was *sustained growth* in the Tigers, China, Southeast Asia, and South Asia (dominated by India) at rates substantially higher than the 2 percent target discussed in chapter 1. Relative to the other regions, South Asia had less robust expansion and Southeast Asia did not bounce back as strongly from the 1997 crisis as did the Tigers. These regions "diverged upwardly" from the rest of the developing world.

The second, slow growth group includes the semi-industrialized countries, Central America and the Caribbean, Central and Eastern Europe, and the Middle Eastern and Northern African region. Many of these countries had grown at fair rates in the 1970s but then experienced a crisis either in the 1980s, the 1990s, or both, followed by growth in the late twentieth and, more commonly, in the early twenty-first century. Over the period 1970–2006, the Central and Eastern European region grew at comparable rates with those recorded by South Asians (2.8 percent vs. 3.0 percent per year), but because of the transition shock around 1990, it seems more appropriate to call its case one of slow growth followed by a late recovery. It must also be mentioned that the recent expansion in the Central and Eastern European countries has benefited a great deal from geopolitical advantages related to their accession to European Union at the beginning of the twenty-first century.

The third group, including the two African regions (with "Other Africa" dominated by Nigeria), the smaller Andean economies, the Middle East and Northern Africa, and Russia and Ukraine, were either *stagnant* throughout the period or experienced volatile economic expansion. Along the lines discussed in chapter 2, data from recent years show that "Representative Africa," Russia and Ukraine, and some of the smaller Andean economies (notably Peru) began to grow again.

Differences in overall growth rates were closely associated with significant changes in the patterns of output growth. Figures 3.2 and 3.3 present scatter plots of per capita GDP growth in agriculture and industry versus the percentage changes in their respective sectoral shares for all the regions. The rapidly growing Asian countries identified in figure 3.1 showed substantial shifts in shares, in the classic movement from primary toward secondary and tertiary sectors.

Figure 3.2 for the agricultural share shows a negatively sloped regression line for the whole 12-region sample. In all regions, except Russia and Ukraine (where agriculture gained less than one percentage point over the period), agriculture tended to grow less than GDP. But contrast the results for the five fast-growing regions with those for the others. While the former show a clear relationship between faster output growth and a decreasing share, the lagging seven regions generate a random scatter—a result that will repeat itself for several other indicators of structural change. Among the rapid growers, China's agricultural share fell by an astonishing 35 percentage points over the period. In South and Southeast Asia, agriculture saw its output share decline 23 percentage points and 17 percentage points, respectively. Similar observations apply to

**FIGURE 3.1**

## Annual growth rate per capita for the three main sectors (1970–2006)

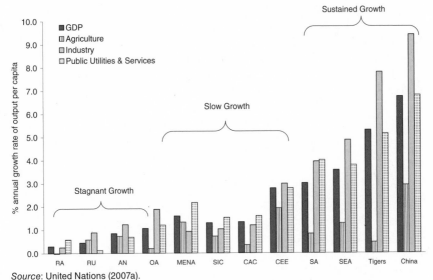

Source: United Nations (2007a).
AN=Andean, CAC=Central America and the Caribbean, CEE=Central and Eastern Europe,
OA= Other Africa, MENA=Middle East and Northern Africa, RA=Representative Africa, RU=Russia
and Ukraine, SA=South Asia, SEA= Southeast Asia, SIC=Semi-industrialized Countries

the industrial sector and service sectors with clear associations emerging for the rapid growers and ill-defined data clouds for the other regions. Growth goes hand in hand with a strong pattern of structural change, whereas the absence of growth does not.

The growing regions had rising industrial shares as can be observed in Figure 3.3 (less so in Central and Eastern Europe, which prior to 1970 had already been aggressively pushed toward industrial specialization). Most of the other regions suffered from stagnation or a reversal of the industrialization process. The Middle Eastern and Northern African countries in fact experienced a decline in the share of the mining sector set off by the OPEC (Organization of the Petroleum Exporting Countries) embargo on crude oil exports to the Western world and the energy crisis of the 1970s. Since then, the region's mining and oil output in total GDP has hovered around 20 percent from a high of 34 percent in 1970.

FIGURE 3.2

## Annual growth rate of GDP per capita and changes in agriculture output share (1970–2006)

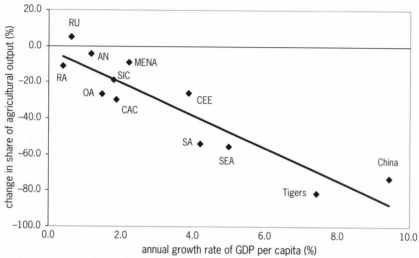

*Source*: United Nations (2007a).

FIGURE 3.3

## Annual growth rate of GDP per capita and changes in industrial output share (1970–2006)

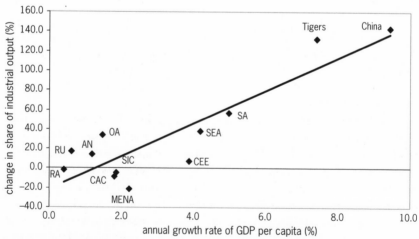

*Source*: United Nations (2007a).

AN=Andean, CAC=Central America and the Caribbean, CEE=Central and Eastern Europe, OA= Other Africa, MENA=Middle East and Northern Africa, RA=Representative Africa, RU=Russia and Ukraine, SA=South Asia, SEA= Southeast Asia, SIC=Semi-industrialized Countries

Finally, the fast growers had predictably large service sector shares by the end of the period, in accordance with traditional development theory. The Tiger region service share, which stood at 57 percent in 2006, supported strong job creation as reported later in this chapter. There was no apparent relationship for the lagging regions.

## Identifying Structural Change

As already suggested by figures 3.2 and 3.3, sustained growth in successful regions was associated with changes in economic structure in several dimensions. Recognizing the structural shifts that occurred in the regions with consistent growth can help chart future directions that other developing economies may be able to take. Needless to say, any economy is a unique entity with its own characteristics that require its own policies. But stylized facts show that there are dynamic movements of key macro variables that show up in connection with sustained output growth across different economic systems. The slow growers did *not* generate such changes for reasons already discussed in chapter 1. Growth over years and decades in per capita output requires economic transformation characterized by higher productivity and increasing returns to scale. The evidence supports this point of view.

Throughout this chapter we analyze these movements from several angles, in terms of formalized decomposition exercises (algebraic details in appendix 3.2) and more informal analysis of data on human capital accumulation and foreign direct investment (FDI).

One decomposition breaks down labor productivity growth between agricultural, industrial (manufacturing, construction, and mining), and service sectors. Overall productivity growth comes out as an average of own rates of growth of the three sectors, weighted by output shares, along with "reallocation effects." These effects are positive for sectors with relatively low average productivity in which employment falls or for high-productivity sectors in which employment rises.[3]

A second exercise focuses on growth rates of the economy-wide employment to population ratio, which is decomposed into an average of growth rates of that ratio in the three sectors weighted by employment shares. At both the national and sectoral levels, the ratio of employment to total population will rise if the growth rate of output per capita exceeds growth of labor productivity.[4] An economy can be considered to be performing well if it has both sustained productivity growth and a stable or rising employment/population ratio.

In a third exercise, we examine the association between capital stock and output growth. We also contrast growth rates of labor and capital productivity and ask how they feed into widely used but fundamentally misleading calculations of total factor productivity growth, or TFPG. A simple accounting identity states that the growth rate of labor productivity is equal to the sum of the growth rates of capital productivity and the capital/labor ratio. The formula helps explain the "Asian" pattern of falling capital productivity over time. As pointed out in chapter 1, a similar identity applies to the growth rates of labor and energy productivity. The details are presented in the following sections.

## Labor Productivity Growth

Historically, labor productivity increases have been the major contributing factor to growth in real GDP per capita. At the same time, faster productivity increases cut into employment growth unless they are offset by rising effective demand. Figure 3.4 shows the direct contribution of each of the three sectors to overall productivity growth for the period 1991–2003/4. The five rapidly growing regions had productivity growth rates exceeding—some to a significant degree—the rich country norm of 2 percent per year. The others fell well short,

**FIGURE 3.4**

### Overall productivity growth and sectoral contributions (1990–2003/4)

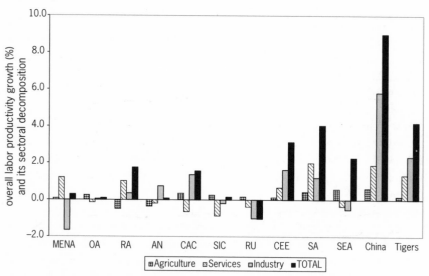

Sources: International Labour Office, GET database, for employment; World Bank, World Development Indicators 2005 database, for output.

Note: The sectoral contribution to overall productivity growth is shown in percentage points. The sum of sectoral percentage points and the reallocation gains, shown in Figure 3.5, equals overall productivity growth.

AN=Andean, CAC=Central America and the Caribbean, CEE=Central and Eastern Europe, OA= Other Africa, MENA=Middle East and Northern Africa, RA=Representative Africa, RU=Russia and Ukraine, SA=South Asia, SEA= Southeast Asia, SIC=Semi-industrialized Countries

FIGURE 3.5

## Sectoral contribution to productivity growth through reallocation gains (1990–2003/4)

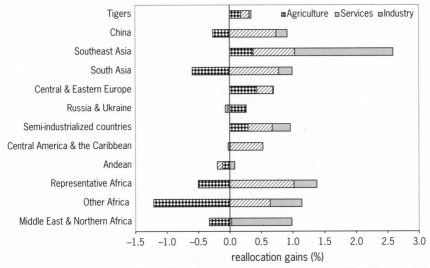

Sources: International Labour Office, GET database, for employment; World Bank, World Development Indicators 2005 database, for output.

and the former USSR had negative productivity growth.[5] Figure 3.5 summarizes sectoral reallocation gains, and together with figure 3.4, it provides a complete picture of how each sector contributed to overall productivity growth.

Productivity growth in the agricultural sector evidently did not play a crucial role in the process. In several countries, agriculture's reallocation effects were negative. The meaning is that this sector, with its relatively low average productivity, had positive employment growth. This finding is not surprising in regions such as China, South Asia, and Africa, where agriculture's share in total employment is significant, but the result is slightly discordant in the Middle East and Northern Africa. More disquieting is the sector's poor productivity performance in sub-Saharan Africa, where it employs most of the labor force.

The industrial sector's own productivity growth made a substantial contribution to the total in four of the rapidly growing regions (figure 3.4). The direct contribution of nearly 6 percent per year in China is striking. Industry made a visible contribution in the two poorer Western Hemisphere regions—Central America and the Caribbean and the Andeans—but detracted from overall performance in the semi-industrialized countries, Russia and Ukraine and the Middle East and Northern Africa. The strongest reallocation contribution of

FIGURE 3.6

**Productivity decomposition for selected Asian regions (1980/6–2000)**

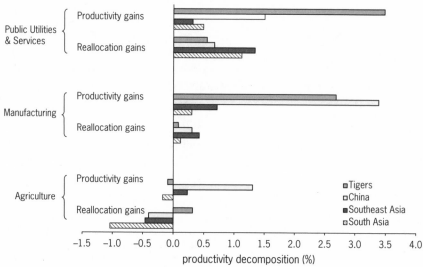

productivity decomposition (%)

*Sources*: Employment data is from the International Centre for the Study of East Asian Development, http://www.icsead.or.jp. Data for sectoral output is from the UN National Accounts database.

industry was experienced in Southeast Asia, a clear outlier in this regard, followed by the Middle East and Northern Africa (figure 3.5).

Services also added to productivity in the rapid growers: as with industry, a negative direct but positive reallocation contribution in Southeast Asia. Elsewhere, the direct contribution from services was typically negative with modest positive contributions from reallocation. This distinction among regions has implications for job creation, as taken up later in this chapter.

Finally, from an alternative data set we were able to do decompositions for the period 1980–2000 for the four Asian regions (1986 as the starting year for South Asia). The results are in figure 3.6. The same general pattern holds as in figures 3.4 and 3.5, with services playing a more important role in the Tigers.

The bottom line on productivity growth is that the two nonagricultural sectors made solid contributions to the total in the fast-growing regions, even as their overall importance in the economy rose. Elsewhere the results were a mixed bag, with no clear patterns emerging. Insofar as it is measured by average labor productivity growth, technological advance was evident in the successful regions and absent or, at best, sporadically present in other corners of the world.

**FIGURE 3.7**

## Economic growth and educational improvements (1970–2000)

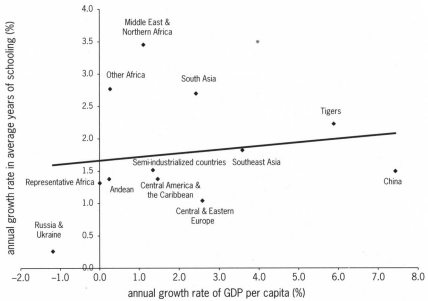

Sources: Data on education is from Barro and Lee (2000), http://www.cid.harvard.edu/ciddata/ciddata
.html. Data on growth rates of GDP per capita is from the UN National Accounts database.

A common route taken by mainstream models of economic growth is to link productivity and ultimately economic growth to the accumulation of human capital. The question to ask is if rapid GDP growth in the regions surveyed in this book was associated with the pace of human capital accumulation, measured by average years of schooling? Figure 3.7 presents a scatter plot of GDP growth per capita versus growth in average years of schooling. All regions raised their education levels, some quite substantially. At best, the regression line suggests a very weak positive relationship (certainly not significant in statistical terms) between output expansion and educational growth. As in figures 3.2 and 3.3, and in contrast to the picture for physical capital accumulation in figure 3.9, the slow-growing regions inhabit an amorphous data cloud. They did no worse at accumulating human capital than the others, but they saw scant returns in growth. In fact some did considerably better at increasing years of schooling than the fastest-growing region, China.

Education is a public good that should be supported for many reasons, but over the medium run its contribution to more rapid real income growth appears to be modest. More human capital may be a necessary or an enabling condition for sustained output growth, but it is clearly not sufficient.

## Employment Growth Patterns

Figure 3.8 summarizes results regarding shifts in sectoral employment to population ratios in terms of their contributions to changes in the economy-wide ratio. Regional growth rates of the overall ratio hovered around zero, with more positive than negative values. As previously noted, at both the sectoral and national levels, the ratio(s) will grow when the growth rate of output per capita exceeds labor productivity growth. The ratio(s) will also tend to rise when population growth is negative, as was the case in Central and Eastern Europe and the former Soviet Union.

The most striking outcome in figure 3.8 is the apparent _similarity_ of all 12 regions in the sense that services showed a rising employment to output ratio everywhere, rather strongly except in Other Africa, the Middle East and Northern Africa, and (to an extent) South Asia (dominated by India). The details, however, differed between fast- and slow-growing regions.

For the rapid growers, the positive contribution of services to employment growth shows that output per capita grew faster than the sector's rising

**FIGURE 3.8**

**Sectoral shifts in employment/population ratios (1991–2003/4)**

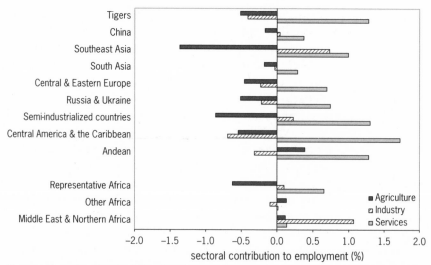

_Sources_: International Labour Office, GET database, for employment; World Bank, World Development Indicators 2005 database, for output.

productivity levels that underlie its positive contributions to growth overall (in figure 3.4). Positive reallocation gains were attributable to the fact that services have relatively high average productivity. In the slower-growing regions, direct contributions of services to economy-wide productivity were generally negative (in five of the seven slow-growth or stagnant regions), indicating that a large part of the job creation in services was in low-productivity or informal activities. Underemployment in services turned out to be the major mechanism to absorb the excess supply of labor in these economies. Still, given the higher average productivity of services, reallocation effects (reflected in figure 3.8) added to overall productivity growth. Only in the Middle East and Northern Africa and in Southeast Asia was the industrial sector a strong provider of jobs (a fact explaining Southeast Asian industry's strong reallocation contribution to overall productivity growth in figure 3.4).

Consistent with figures 3.1 and 3.4, industry's rate of productivity growth tended to exceed its growth in demand per capita. An old structuralist observation in development economics is that the industrial sector is the main motor for productivity increases but not for job creation.

Finally, relative to total population, agriculture was a net source of labor *supply* in nine regions, very strongly in Southeast Asia, and a source of net demand—or, to be precise, an absorber of underemployment—in the Middle East and Northern Africa, Other Africa, and (especially) in the smaller Andean countries.

## *Capital Productivity and Total Factor Productivity Growth*

To analyze the role of capital accumulation in growth, we computed capital stock growth rates for the regions by cumulating real gross fixed capital formation over time from a postulated initial level of the capital stock (capital/output ratio of 2.5) with a depreciation rate of 5 percent. As discussed more fully in appendix 3.2, after a decade or two such estimates of the capital growth rate should be insensitive to the parameters because capital stock growth tends to converge to investment growth over time.[6]

Figure 3.9 compares growth rates of output and the capital stock. In contrast to most other indicators discussed, there is a clear positive association between the two growth rates across *all* regions—a standard empirical result. This relationship is usually thought to emerge from the supply side, but it could also be attributed to demand. In a simple demand-driven growth model, if investment increases at a certain rate, then output and (as just indicated) the capital stock will ultimately grow at that rate as well. The fact that the slope of the putative relationship between the two growth rates in figure 3.9 is close to one argues more for demand- than supply-side causality. In the latter, the slope would lie below 45 degrees, with a less than one-for-one partial impact of faster capital growth on output growth.[7]

Also note that the capital growth rate exceeded output growth in the Tigers, China, Southeast Asia, and the former USSR. In other words, these

FIGURE 3.9

## Growth rates of output and capital stock (1990–2004)

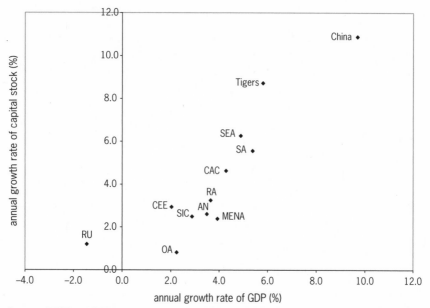

Sources: GFCF and GDP data comes from World Bank, World Development Indicators 2005 database; employment data is from the International Labour Office, GET database.

AN=Andean, CAC=Central America and the Caribbean, CEE=Central and Eastern Europe, OA=Other Africa, MENA=Middle East and Northern Africa, RA=Representative Africa, RU=Russia and Ukraine, SA=South Asia, SIC=Semi-industrialized Countries

regions had *falling* capital productivity. Such an outcome can be expected in the rapidly growing Asian regions where industrial restructuring took place toward capital-intensive industries. Nevertheless these findings can also be said to be the outcome of accounting requirements. As noted in chapter 1 and demonstrated in appendix 3.2, a theorem of accounting demonstrates that the difference between labor and capital productivity growth rates must be equal to the difference between capital and labor growth rates. If capital grows faster than labor, then labor productivity has to grow faster than capital productivity.[8] If the capital to labor ratio rises very rapidly, then capital productivity growth may even have to be negative. This outcome is sometimes said to characterize an "Asian" pattern of growth, or a "Marx bias" in technical progress. It can also result from negative labor force growth as in the former USSR and Eastern Europe.

Capital and labor productivity growth rates are plotted in figure 3.10. Again note the contrast between regions. The rapid growers all had negative or nearly zero capital productivity growth rates and rising labor productivity, which could have resulted from better technology "embodied" in new capital goods. Detailed data show that China's capital productivity fell more rapidly over time. The former USSR lost on both fronts and the rest had small, mostly positive, growth of both indicators.

Much of the academic literature focuses on total factor productivity growth or the "residual." In chapter 1, we pointed out the dubious way in which the share of remunerated labor is calculated in developing countries and the equally inadequate interpretation of a negative TFPG in rapidly growing economies. As an exercise, figure 3.10 shows estimates of TFPG for labor shares of 0.4 and 0.7 (the standard number), respectively. Either way, because of their negative capital productivity growth, TFPG in the rapidly growing regions fell well short of labor productivity growth. For the lower labor share, TFPG in the Tigers and Southeast Asia was close to zero. Such findings are often used to portray the failings of the "Asian model," but mostly they reflect an accounting identity and the arbitrary nature of the TFPG indicator.

A more interesting question would be to ask whether the rapid growth of the capital stock in these economies impacted labor productivity through embodied technical change (and the slow growth of the capital stock therefore led to the poor productivity performance of other regions), but this is a question we cannot directly address with our data set.

What we can ask, however, is whether foreign direct investment, which is often touted as a potential source of technologically upgraded physical capital, managerial know-how, and global commercial networks, has any impact on productivity and economic growth. However, it is not obvious in this regard what level of FDI is "significant." As a share of GDP, for example, how large does FDI have to be or how rapidly should it grow to generate important repercussions on output growth?

FDI tends to fluctuate over time although as a share of GDP it remains insignificant or modest at best in most of the developing world. More exactly, for the fast-growing Tigers, FDI as a share of GDP increased from 1.6 percent in 1970 to 3.1 percent by 2004. Somewhat similar patterns appeared in Southeast Asia and China—which absorbed a very substantial share of the worldwide total—but not in South Asia, where FDI/GDP peaked at a mere 0.9 percent in 1997. Central and Eastern Europe experienced a late but sharper increase of FDI as a share of GDP than Southeastern Asia: from 0.4 percent in 1990 to 4.8 percent in 2000 and 4 percent in 2004. Russia received relatively little FDI: it peaked at 1.7 percent of GDP in 1999.

Central America and the Caribbean had strong fluctuations—nearly 4 percent in the 1970s down to 0.4 percent in 1982, back to above 4 percent in the 1990s with the assembly and tourism boom, and then some decline. Latin America saw a modest 2 percent toward the end of the period. Some members

**FIGURE 3.10**

## Capital and labor productivity growth rates and TFPG (1991–2004) when labor share is 0.4 (upper diagram) and 0.7 (lower diagram) respectively.

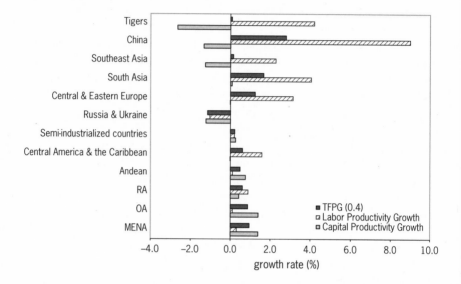

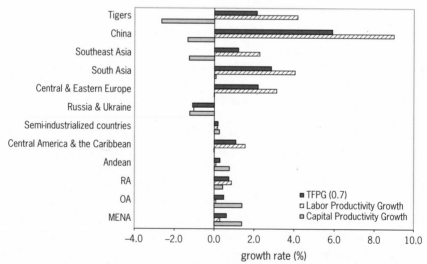

*Sources*: GFCF and GDP data comes from World Bank, World Development Indicators 2005 database; employment data is from the International Labour Office, GET database.

of the slow-growing group of economies did similarly or a little better than the fast growers in garnering FDI, without a lot of apparent payoff. The smaller Andean countries were up to 5.5 percent in 1993 and 3 percent in 2004, with no positive impact on growth. Finally, Africa and the Middle East and Northern Africa got negligible quantities of FDI.

This narrative on the shares of FDI in GDP reveals that a positively sloped relationship between FDI and GDP growth is likely to show up for Asia, as usual—with the exception of South Asia in this case. The remaining regions demonstrate their usual blob of data points. A relatively large FDI inflow may possibly have a slightly stronger association with growth than rising education, but the relationship is still very weak.

## Energy Productivity Growth and Energy/Labor Ratios

An old idea, which perhaps dates to the nineteenth century "energetics" movement (Martinez-Alier with Schlüpmann 1991; Mirowski 1989), is that the crucial factor behind rising labor productivity and per capita income is increasing use of energy. One can make this statement a bit more precise by comparing growth rates of labor productivity, energy productivity, and the energy/labor ratio. As previously noted, the latter two growth rates must add up to the first as an algebraic identity.

For our 12 regional groups and the rich countries in the OECD, figure 3.11 presents two scatter diagrams of growth rates of labor productivity and the energy/labor ratio, for the periods 1970–1990 and 1990–2004 (energy from fossil fuel sources only). As with the growth rate of capital stock, there appears to be a positive relationship between increasing energy use per worker and labor productivity growth, with a steeper slope and a better fit in the latter period. Similar results show up when growth rates are compared at the individual country level. The slope of the relationship in the latter period is around 0.6, implying a substantial contribution of more energy use to higher labor productivity.

The data behind figure 3.11 show a wide range of annual energy/labor ratios—from 0.01 (77 gallons of gasoline) in sub-Saharan Africa to 0.67 (5150 gallons) in Saudi Arabia in 2004. The ratio is 0.58 in the United States and less than 0.3 in Western European countries, the Tigers, and Japan (as discussed in chapter 1, the numbers are in units of terajoules of energy per worker per year).

In the context of global warming, the numbers are far from encouraging. For example, at China's growth rate of the energy/labor ratio of 4 percent per year, it would take the economy around 35 years to attain Sweden's "moderate" ratio of 0.16, with energy productivity rising 4 percent per year more slowly than labor productivity. As its per capita income rises and possibilities for appropriating more advanced technologies and taking advantage of surplus labor recede, China's labor productivity growth rate will almost certainly decline, perhaps creating even greater reliance on energy.

FIGURE 3.11

## Growth rates of labor productivity and the energy/labor ratio

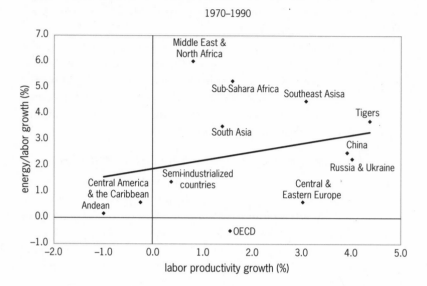

1970–1990

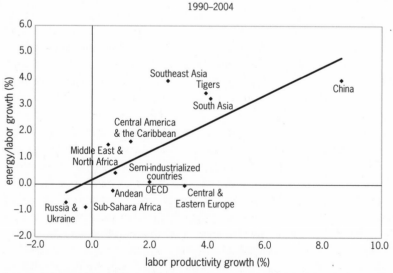

1990–2004

*Sources*: Energy data are from the UN Energy Statistics Yearbook, GDP levels are from the UN National Accounts, and employment data are from Groningen Growth and Development Center, http://www.ggdc.net.

As observed in chapter 1, developing countries might have to reduce their fossil fuel energy/labor ratios by 1 percent per year to hold greenhouse gas emissions in check. A handful of countries are in this range, but they are stagnant with negligible or negative labor productivity growth.

The key policy question is whether in the near future rich country energy/labor ratios can be reduced (or energy productivity increased relative to labor productivity) substantially by technological innovation and social rearrangements. In the recent period, there has been no significant downward trend in the ratios in the industrialized world. But if such innovations do work out, then perhaps they can be passed to developing economies before the momentum of their population growth overwhelms all possibilities for combating global warming. Given the environmental constraints and considering that only 16 percent of the world's population lives in rich countries and almost all population growth is in the poor ones, realistic prospects for successful economic performance and poverty alleviation may not be very bright.

## APPENDIX 3.1:
## COUNTRIES IN THE REGIONAL GROUPS

1. Representative Africa: Ghana, Kenya, Uganda, and Tanzania

2. Other Africa: Cameroon, Ethiopia, Ivory Coast, Mozambique, Nigeria, and Zimbabwe

3. Central America and the Caribbean: Costa Rica, Dominican Republic, El Salvador, Guatemala, and Jamaica

4. Smaller Andean countries: Bolivia, Ecuador, and Peru

5. Semi-industrialized countries: Argentina, Brazil, Chile, Colombia, Mexico, Venezuela, Turkey, and South Africa

6. South Asia: Bangladesh, India, Pakistan, and Sri Lanka

7. China

8. Southeast Asia: Indonesia, Philippines, Thailand, and Vietnam

9. Tigers: South Korea, Malaysia, Singapore, and Taiwan

10. Middle East and Northern Africa: Algeria, Egypt, Morocco, Tunisia, Iran, Iraq, Jordan, Saudi Arabia, Syria, and Yemen

11. Former USSR: Russian Federation, and Ukraine

12. Eastern Europe: Bulgaria, Czech Republic, Hungary, Poland, Romania, and Slovakia

# APPENDIX 3.2:
# DECOMPOSITION TECHNIQUES

It is often illuminating to trace through how macro aggregates shift over time by temporally "decomposing" accounting identities that link them together. In this appendix, we present procedures for investigating changes in labor productivity across producing sectors, employment generation by sectors and interactions between labor and capital productivity growth at the economy-wide level.[9]

Available data on output and employment come at yearly intervals. Growth rates have to be computed in discrete time, with formulas that can become quite complicated. To simplify an algebraic presentation as much as possible, we consider only observations at times 0 and 1. The growth rate of, say, the variable $X$ is "X-hat" or $\hat{X} = (X_1 - X_0)/X_0$ with the subscripts standing for points in time. At time 0, the relevant identity for decomposing labor productivity growth is $\sum_i X_0^i = X_0$ with the $X_0^i$ as output levels by sector ($i = 1, 2, \ldots, n$). Let $\theta_0^i = X_0^i/X_0$ be the share of sector $i$ in real output in period zero. Similarly for employment: $\varepsilon_0^i = L_0^i/L_0$ with $\sum_i L_0^i = L_0$. The level of labor productivity in sector $i$ is $X_0^i/L_0^i$ with an exact growth rate between times 0 and 1 being

$$\xi_L^i = (1 + \hat{L}^i)^{-1}(\hat{X}^i - \hat{L}^i) \approx \bar{X}^i - \hat{L}^i.$$

In the literature, terms such as $(1 + \hat{L})^{-1}$ are often said to represent "interactions."

After a bit of manipulation, an exact expression for the rate of growth of economy-wide labor productivity emerges as

$$\xi_L = (1 + \hat{L})^{-1}\sum_i[\theta_0^i(\hat{X}^i - \hat{L}^i) + (\theta_0^i - \varepsilon_0^i)\hat{L}^i]. \tag{1}$$

Aside from the interaction term $(1 + \hat{L})^{-1}$, $\xi_L$ decomposes into two parts. One is a weighted average $\sum_i\theta_0^i(\hat{X}^i - \hat{L}^i)$ of sectoral rates of productivity growth as conventionally measured. The weights are the output shares $\theta_0^i$. The other term, $\sum_i(\theta_0^i - \varepsilon_0^i)\hat{L}^i$, captures "reallocation effects." If $\theta_0^i > \varepsilon_0^i$ sector $i$ has a bigger share in output than employment, implying that it has relatively high average productivity. Positive employment growth in that sector (or a negative $\hat{L}^i$ in a sector with $\theta_0^i < \varepsilon_0^i$) will increase productivity overall, in line with established theories about dualism in development economics.

For the record, another expression for $\xi_L$ emerges after rearrangement of (1),

$$\xi_L = (1 + \hat{L})^{-1}\sum_i[\varepsilon_0^i(\hat{X}^i - \hat{L}^i) + (\theta_0^i - \varepsilon_0^i)\hat{X}^i]. \tag{2}$$

In (2), sectoral productivity growth rates are weighted by employment shares, and the reallocation effect is stated in terms of output growth rates. The message is basically the same as in (1).

Turning to employment generation, a fundamental insight is that if a sector creates jobs over time, then (if interaction terms are ignored) its growth rate of output per capita must exceed its growth rate of labor productivity. To see the details we can start with the identity $\phi_0 = L_0/P_0 = \sum_i (L_0^i/X_0^i)(X_0^i/P_0)$, in which $P_0$ is the population at time zero. That is, $\phi_0$ is the share of the population employed at time 0. Labor/output ratios (inverse average productivity levels) by sector are $b_0^i = L_0^i/X_0^i$ and sectoral output levels per capita are $\chi_0^i = X_0^i/P_0$. After grinding, the growth rate of $\phi$ can be expressed as

$$\hat{\phi} = \sum_i \varepsilon_0^i (\hat{\chi}^i + \hat{b}^i + \hat{\chi}^i \hat{b}^i),$$

with the $\varepsilon_0^i$ being the sectoral employment shares introduced above and $\hat{\chi}^i \hat{b}^i$ as a (presumably small) interaction term. Each sector's growth rate of labor productivity is $\xi_L^i = (1 + \hat{L}^i)^{-1}(\hat{X}^i - \hat{L}^i)$, so that it is related to the growth rate of the labor/output ratio as $\hat{b}^i(1 + \hat{X}^i) = -\xi_L^i(1 + \hat{L}^i)$. A final expression for $\hat{\phi}$ becomes

$$\hat{\phi} = \sum_i \varepsilon_0^i [\hat{\chi}^i - \xi_L^i (1 + \hat{\chi}^i)(1 + \hat{L}^i)(1 + \hat{X}^i)^{-1}], \tag{3}$$

with the terms multiplying $\xi_L^i$ capturing the interactions.

The lead term (typically accurate to two or three significant digits) is

$$\hat{\phi} = \sum_i \varepsilon_0^i (\hat{\chi}^i - \xi_L^i).$$

The growth rate of the employment/population ratio is a weighted average of differences between sectoral growth rates of output per capita and productivity. Sectors with higher shares of total employment $\varepsilon_0^i$ contribute more strongly to the average. One might expect that $\hat{\chi}_i > \xi_L^i$ in a "dynamic" sector, with the inequality reversed in one that is "declining" or just "mature."

Next we consider labor and capital productivity in tandem on an economy-wide basis. Exact expressions for the growth rates of the two variables are $\xi_L = (1 + \hat{L})^{-1}(\hat{X} - \hat{L}) \approx \hat{X} - \hat{L}$ and $\xi_K = (1 + \hat{K})^{-1}(\hat{X} - \hat{K}) \approx \hat{X} - \hat{K}$. The growth of capital stock is given by the standard equation $\hat{K} = (I_0/K_0) - \delta$, in which $I_0$ is gross fixed capital formation and $\delta$ is a "radioactive" depreciation rate (approximately equal to the inverse of the average lifetime of a capital good).

We estimated the capital stock growth rates used in the text by running the accumulation equation forward through time from an initial guess at the level of capital (from a capital to output ratio of 2.5) and a depreciation rate of 0.05. After a decade or so, the computed growth rates were insensitive to these parameters. This outcome is more or less built into the algebra. If investment grows at a rate $g$, for example, then the capital stock growth rate will converge to that value, independent of initial conditions and the value of $\delta$.

Usually, labor and capital productivity growth rates are lumped together into a number called total factor productivity growth (TFPG) or, more realistically, the "residual" $\xi$. It is defined by the equation

$$\hat{X} = \alpha_0(\hat{L} + \xi_L) + (1 - \alpha_0)(\hat{K} + \xi_K) = \alpha_0\hat{L} + (1 - \alpha_0)\hat{K} + \xi, \qquad (4)$$

in which $\alpha_0$ is the share of labor in total factor payments. Evidently, $\xi$ is a weighted average of capital and labor productivity growth rates,

$$\xi = \alpha_0\xi_L + (1 - \alpha_0)\xi_K. \qquad (5)$$

Equation (4) can be derived by taking the first difference of the factor payments identity built into the national accounts, $X_0 = \omega_0 L_0 + r_0 K_0$ (in which $\omega_0$ and $r_0$ are real wage and profit rates, respectively), or else from the usual mainstream mumbo jumbo about an aggregate production function and associated marginal productivity factor demand equations.

Also, because

$$\frac{X_0/L_0}{X_0/K_0} = \frac{K_0}{L_0}$$

the expression

$$\xi_L - \xi_K = \hat{K} - \hat{L} \qquad (6)$$

will hold to a good approximation. In other words, if growth rates of labor and capital are predetermined, then the growth rate of labor productivity implies the growth rate of capital productivity or vice versa. If capital grows much more rapidly than labor and there is positive labor productivity growth, then the growth rate of capital productivity may well be negative. Empirical implications of this observation are discussed in the text of this chapter.

One final point worth emphasizing is that all the discussion is framed in terms of macro aggregates measured in real market prices, *not* in terms of purchasing power parity. The rationale is to keep the analysis as close as possible to normal macroeconomic discourse.

When used in international comparisons, PPP calculations basically revalue the labor content of output by sector. For example, the dollar cost of an upmarket haircut in Mumbai at the current rupee/dollar exchange rate might be $5. A similar service in New York City could run $50. A PPP recomputation of Indian GDP raises the labor cost for the Mumbai barber to something closer to that of the New York counterpart.

Comparisons of income levels in these terms have become the accepted methodology, as in the results reported in figure 2.1. However, PPP computations also move macro aggregates far away from their "normal" market price levels. Nontraded goods are revalued in comparison to traded goods, the residential capital stock rises and nonresidential falls, imports change relative to exports, and so on. In the text of this chapter, we focus on standard macroeconomics, and for that reason we eschew PPP.

## Notes

1. The representative group is made up of four countries often discussed in the development literature, and the others are included essentially on grounds of data availability.
2. We use here data in constant U.S. dollars rather than in the purchasing power parity (PPP) terms customarily utilized in international income comparisons (as, for example, in chapter 2). The reason, as explained in appendix 3.2, is that PPP estimates distort the macroeconomic relationships that are at the heart of our analysis in this and the following chapters. When it comes to policy formation, it is far more useful to think about macro relationships in traditional "real" terms (for a discussion of "real" terms, see chapter 1).
3. The approach follows Syrquin (1986).
4. The original insight is Pasinetti's (1981). The decomposition holds true if labor force participation rates are stable.
5. More detailed results (not presented) show that Russia/Ukraine suffered an enormous productivity collapse (−9.7 percent per year) in 1991–1995 but then recovered to 5.6 percent (1999–2003).
6. A caveat: our capital stock series for the former USSR and Central and Eastern Europe begin in 1990, which means that the estimated growth rates are less reliable than those for other regions where the base year was 1970.
7. That is, the 45-degree slope would not fit a neoclassical aggregate production function. It could be "explained" by a constant capital/output ratio, but that in turn is inconsistent with the "Asian" pattern of falling capital productivity discussed in this section.
8. This sort of "decreasing returns" to more capital is built into many mainstream and heterodox growth models, which mostly serve to rationalize the accounting identity described in the text. As noted in chapter 1, falling capital productivity (in PPP terms) characterized many now industrialized countries in their rapid growth periods in the nineteenth and early twentieth centuries.
9. More detail on the analysis to follow is in Rada and Taylor (2006) and Taylor and Rada (2007).

# CHAPTER 4

# Open Economies and Patterns of Trade

## (WITH MARIÁNGELA PARRA)

THIS CHAPTER takes up the relationship between foreign trade and growth in developing countries in the latter part of the twentieth century. Regional diversity was again the rule, with changing patterns of trade accompanying structural transformation. Fast-growing regions generally recorded increases in shares of manufactured exports with mid- and high-technological content, the most impressive being the Tigers and, in its speed of transformation, China. Recently in some countries, economic growth has been associated with specialization in dynamic services such as information and communications technologies, with India standing out in this area. In the slow-growing regions on the other hand, trade diversification and technological upgrading were far less evident. The slow growers were also subject to terms of trade and other external shocks.

For orthodox economists, openness to trade is an important explanatory factor for economic growth. Higher growth rates are supposed to be spurred by "gains from trade" attributable to access to lower-cost foreign products and more efficient domestic resource allocation on the supply side. True to their mercantilist heritage, structuralists point out that exports can stimulate domestic production through the multiplier. Also, as discussed in chapter 1, access to foreign exchange from exports can be used to import necessary products to satisfy demand. Imported foreign technology can lead to better and more productive investment that taps potential increasing returns to scale.

In the discussion to follow, we first take up the changes in the pattern of trade in goods and services, and the evolution of the terms of trade of commodities. We then explore the links between specialization patterns and economic performance and conclude with some policy implications, which are developed further in the following chapters.

# Changing Patterns of Trade

Over the long term, all countries included in Maddison's (2001) data set had positive growth rates in the value of merchandise exports. As a share of GDP, exports generally have increased since the nineteenth century (figure 4.1). This process has been, of course, far from monotonic, with a general reversal during the interwar period of the twentieth century and specific regional reversals in other periods.

The usual long-run conclusion drawn is that there are positive effects of trade expansion on overall labor productivity. Over given periods, however, the relationship may not be present. For example, in the 1990s greater trade openness was *not* associated with faster economy-wide productivity in most countries. As emphasized in chapter 1, not just openness to trade but a nation's "insertion" into the global economic system (aid and debt relationships, patterns of trade, commodity price shifts, and access to technology) strongly conditions its prospects.

Since the 1960s, growth in trade has been accompanied by a gradual change in the specialization patterns of developing countries away from primary commodities. This process accelerated after the 1980s but was very uneven across the developing world (Lall 2001, chap. 4; Akyüz 2003, chap. 1; Ocampo and Vos 2008, chap. 3). Table 4.1 summarizes the patterns of transformation of the export structure in the different regions defined in the previous chapter. We use the late Sanjaya Lall's well-known classification of the technological and natural resource content of merchandise exports.

**FIGURE 4.1**

**Merchandise exports as percent of GDP by regions (1870–1998)**

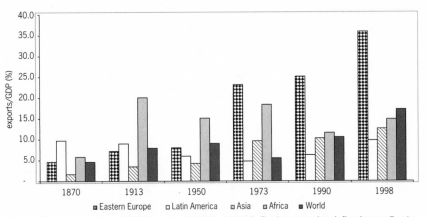

*Sources*: Data on exports and GDP are from Maddison (2001). Regions are also defined according to Maddison (2001).

**TABLE 4.1**

## Shares of Commodities with Different Technological Content as a Percent of Total Exports

### Tigers

| Period | 1985–1986 | 1990–1991 | 1995–1996 | 2000–2001 | 2005–2006 |
|---|---|---|---|---|---|
| Primary products | 14 | 7 | 5 | 4 | 4 |
| Resource-based manufactures | 20 | 14 | 10 | 10 | 14 |
| Low-technology manufactures | 23 | 27 | 17 | 14 | 11 |
| Medium-technology manufactures | 23 | 25 | 26 | 25 | 27 |
| High-technology manufactures | 17 | 27 | 40 | 46 | 42 |
| Others | 3 | 1 | 2 | 1 | 2 |

### China

| Period | 1985–1986 | 1990–1991 | 1995–1996 | 2000–2001 | 2005–2006 |
|---|---|---|---|---|---|
| Primary products | 56 | 19 | 10 | 7 | 4 |
| Resource-based manufactures | 15 | 11 | 11 | 9 | 8 |
| Low-technology manufactures | 21 | 42 | 46 | 40 | 31 |
| Medium-technology manufactures | 6 | 21 | 18 | 20 | 22 |
| High-technology manufactures | 1 | 6 | 14 | 23 | 34 |
| Others | 0 | 2 | 1 | 1 | 1 |

### Semi-industrialized countries

| Period | 1985–1986 | 1990–1991 | 1995–1996 | 2000–2001 | 2005–2006 |
|---|---|---|---|---|---|
| Primary products | 44 | 43 | 29 | 24 | 30 |
| Resource-based manufactures | 25 | 20 | 19 | 16 | 16 |
| Low-technology manufactures | 13 | 14 | 15 | 14 | 12 |

### Southeast Asia

| Period | 1985–1986 | 1990–1991 | 1995–1996 | 2000–2001 | 2005–2006 |
|---|---|---|---|---|---|
| Primary products | 57 | 34 | 23 | 20 | 21 |
| Resource-based manufactures | 20 | 21 | 19 | 15 | 18 |
| Low-technology manufactures | 10 | 24 | 22 | 19 | 16 |
| Medium-technology manufactures | 5 | 9 | 13 | 15 | 19 |
| High-technology manufactures | 2 | 10 | 19 | 29 | 25 |
| Others | 5 | 3 | 4 | 2 | 1 |

### South Asia

| Period | 1985–1986 | 1990–1991 | 1995–1996 | 2000–2001 | 2005–2006 |
|---|---|---|---|---|---|
| Primary products | 30 | 20 | 18 | 13 | 12 |
| Resource-based manufactures | 21 | 19 | 19 | 21 | 32 |
| Low-technology manufactures | 39 | 47 | 48 | 48 | 34 |
| Medium-technology manufactures | 6 | 9 | 10 | 10 | 15 |
| High-technology manufactures | 2 | 3 | 4 | 5 | 5 |
| Others | 1 | 2 | 1 | 2 | 1 |

### Andean countries

| Period | 1985–1986 | 1990–1991 | 1995–1996 | 2000–2001 | 2005–2006 |
|---|---|---|---|---|---|
| Primary products | 66 | 67 | 63 | 55 | 51 |
| Resource-based manufactures | 27 | 24 | 21 | 22 | 29 |
| Low-technology manufactures | 4 | 8 | 7 | 9 | 6 |

| | Medium-technology manufactures | High-technology manufactures | Others |
|---|---|---|---|
| | 14 | 3 | 1 |
| | 18 | 3 | 1 |
| | 26 | 9 | 1 |
| | 27 | 16 | 3 |
| | 25 | 11 | 5 |
| | 2 | 0 | 1 |
| | 1 | 0 | 0 |
| | 2 | 1 | 6 |
| | 3 | 1 | 10 |
| | 3 | 1 | 11 |

| | Central America and the Caribbean | | | | | Central and Eastern Europe | | | | |
|---|---|---|---|---|---|---|---|---|---|---|
| Primary products | 56 | 44 | 34 | 29 | 25 | 28 | 21 | 12 | 7 | 7 |
| Resource-based manufactures | 27 | 31 | 21 | 24 | 26 | 10 | 19 | 20 | 15 | 15 |
| Low-technology manufactures | 8 | 12 | 15 | 16 | 18 | 17 | 23 | 31 | 26 | 20 |
| Medium-technology manufactures | 4 | 6 | 10 | 13 | 14 | 28 | 26 | 29 | 36 | 39 |
| High-technology manufactures | 4 | 4 | 3 | 17 | 16 | 13 | 6 | 7 | 14 | 16 |
| Others | 0 | 3 | 17 | 1 | 1 | 5 | 5 | 1 | 2 | 3 |

| | Former USSR | | | | | Representative Africa | | | | |
|---|---|---|---|---|---|---|---|---|---|---|
| Primary products | 12 | 18 | 39 | 44 | 49 | 67 | 50 | 55 | 51 | 41 |
| Resource-based manufactures | 19 | 17 | 19 | 19 | 23 | 23 | 28 | 22 | 19 | 25 |
| Low-technology manufactures | 2 | 3 | 8 | 7 | 5 | 4 | 12 | 8 | 6 | 5 |
| Medium-technology manufactures | 8 | 3 | 17 | 14 | 13 | 3 | 8 | 4 | 2 | 4 |
| High-technology manufactures | 60 | 59 | 3 | 4 | 2 | 1 | 1 | 1 | 1 | 1 |
| Others | — | — | 15 | 11 | 8 | 1 | 2 | 11 | 20 | 24 |

| | Other Africa | | | | | Middle East and Northern Africa | | | | |
|---|---|---|---|---|---|---|---|---|---|---|
| Primary products | 65 | 90 | 76 | 90 | 55 | 70 | 72 | 68 | 74 | 77 |
| Resource-based manufactures | 18 | 3 | 14 | 6 | 28 | 21 | 15 | 17 | 13 | 11 |
| Low-technology manufactures | 5 | 2 | 4 | 1 | 2 | 5 | 6 | 8 | 6 | 4 |
| Medium-technology manufactures | 9 | 3 | 4 | 2 | 9 | 4 | 6 | 6 | 5 | 6 |
| High-technology manufactures | 1 | 0 | 0 | 0 | 1 | 0 | 1 | 1 | 1 | 1 |
| Others | 1 | 1 | 1 | 1 | 5 | 0 | 0 | 0 | 1 | 1 |

Source: Authors' calculations based on UN-COMTRADE (2008) online database. Classifications based on Lall (2001).

The rapidly growing regions in Asia had the most significant shifts in technological content—although less so in South Asia than in the other three. As noted above, the Tiger economies led in terms of technologically advanced exports, which reached 40 percent or more of total exports since the mid-1990s. Their medium-technology exports largely maintained their share, whereas the low-technology and natural resource–based components (both primary goods and resource-based manufactures) dropped off sharply.

Southeast Asia followed a similar but slower pattern of transformation. Reflecting its relatively richer endowment, as compared to other Asian regions, its resource-based exports held up much more than in the Tigers and still represented close to two-fifths of total exports in the mid-2000s. The region saw, in any case, a sharp increase in the export share of mid- and high-tech exports, which jointly increased in 1985–1986 from 7 percent of total exports of goods to 44 percent in 2005–2006. Some of these exports, particularly those of high technology, have a strong dependence on manufacturing assembly operations, with domestic value-added in the range of 10–20 percent of the value of exports.

Trade patterns also shifted to a significant degree toward manufactures and away from primary products in the South Asian countries, largely driven by trends in India. These economies remained, however, at the lower end of the technological content of exports, although gradually moving up and accompanied, in the case of India—though not the neighboring countries—by a boom of "dynamic services" (see this topic later in the chapter). In 2005–2006 South Asia still overwhelmingly specialized in exporting resource-based or low-tech commodities, which made up about 80 percent of its export basket of goods. This slower transformation also included limited expansion of assembly operations in India and Pakistan, which were more important in Sri Lanka and Bangladesh.

Even if compared to its successful regional counterparts, the export transformation of China was particularly impressive. From a structure not very different from that of Southeast Asia in the mid-1980s, it moved to one closer to that of the Tigers two decades later. China's exports of high-technology manufactures rose from 1 percent of the total exports in 1985–1986 to 34 percent in 2005–2006, whereas the share of mid-technology goods increased from 6 to 22 percent. Low-tech manufactures remained relatively important, however, indeed closer to the patterns of South Asia, whereas resource-based exports decreased sharply. Although the assembly activities peculiar to late twentieth-century globalization constitute an important part of its export structure, the Chinese economy has clearly compensated for dependence on imported components with a broad industrial export dynamism, as reflected in its large manufacturing export surplus. There has been a growing deficit in mining (including energy) products, thus generating growing linkages with the natural resource–based economies in other regions of the developing world.[1]

The semi-industrialized countries also recorded an increase in the share of manufacturing exports, but the speed of this transformation was slow relative to that of all the Asian regions. This trend did not offset the region's historical pattern of specialization as a net importer of manufactured goods and a net exporter of agriculture and mining. Reflecting abundant natural endowments, 46 percent of the region's total exports were still resource-based in 2005–2006. With some important exceptions (Mexico's incursion into high-technology activities with a large assembly component), the mid-tech manufactures were relatively more successful. Some of these industries—such as automobiles and process industries—had grown up under import substitution and made a successful transformation into export markets.

The smaller Andean economies remained poorly articulated into the global trading system. Table 4.1 shows that around 80 percent of the region's exports were still made up of primary commodities or natural resource–based manufactures in the mid-2000s. In contrast, the Central America and the Caribbean economies fared better in exporting (largely assembled) manufactured goods as well as tourist services (see this topic later in this chapter). The surge in high-technology exports in this group has a single explanation: Intel's production of computer chips in Costa Rica, with limited domestic content. More generally, the region remained a net importer of manufactures throughout the entire period, indicating that assembly exports did not generate the type of dynamic industrial linkages observed in the Asian economies undergoing similar transformations.

Central and Eastern European exports have been dominated since the 1980s by manufactures, basically as a consequence of the rapid industrialization policies followed after World War II and based on the Soviet model and supported by the Council for Mutual Economic Assistance (COMECOM). This pattern of specialization implied a chronic deficit of mining and energy products, fitting the energy-intensive nature of Soviet-style technologies. As a share of total exports, high-tech products in Central and Eastern Europe were below that of the Tigers in the mid-1980s and also below those of China and Southeast Asia in the mid-2000s. This finding confirms Podkaminer's (2006) observation that a structural mistake was made during the "planned" years in that not enough attention was paid to specialization in high-technology sectors. As in the semi-industrialized countries of Latin America, Turkey, and South Africa, it was more the mid-technology sectors that led the transformation of the export structure.

Whereas the transition implied for Central and Eastern Europe the deepening of the previous industrialization process, for the former USSR it implied a veritable "reprimarization" of its export structure. The data in table 4.1 apply only to Russia and Ukraine but are representative for the former USSR as a whole. The Russian Federation has become primarily an exporter of mining, particularly energy-related products (oil and natural gas), with the share of primary commodities increasing from 12 percent in 1985–1986 to 49 percent in 2005–2006—or from 31 percent to 72 percent if natural resource based manufactures are included.

An even higher and stable dependence on exports of natural resources is typical of most of the selected Middle Eastern and North African economies. In total, about 90 percent of exports in this region are either primary commodities or natural resource–based manufactures. It should be underlined that these results can be attributed to the large share of Saudi Arabia in the region's total exports. The aggregation then overshadows the trade patterns for smaller countries such as Tunisia, Jordan, and Morocco, which now export mostly manufacturing products and tourist services.

Finally, we can look at how sub-Saharan Africa is performing in terms of integration into the global trading system. As can be observed in table 4.1, the two subregions exported mostly resource-based and low-tech products. The larger medium-tech share in Other Africa is driven by Zimbabwe's exports (as of 2008 strongly affected by ongoing political turmoil), while the Representative Africa region records a slightly higher range of low-tech manufactures.

## Trade in Services

With new information and communication technologies spreading worldwide, the transfer of some service activities across countries and continents has become feasible. The Internet revolution of the 1990s played a crucial role in this transfer. An important outcome has been the outsourcing of back-office services from developed to developing economies.

The most publicized case is that of India. An English-speaking, educated labor force attracted many multinational corporations that transferred part of their operations to take advantage of lower labor costs. An immediate question is whether these service activities can contribute, by themselves, to dynamic growth in the Hirschmanian sense of establishing linkages with other domestic sectors or in the Kaldorian sense of inducing productivity change. More directly, in what way do the calling centers outsourced by U.S. firms to Bangalore contribute to the establishment of new economic activities, besides those resulting from the final demand by the employed labor? An industrial sector would do that through demand for intermediate inputs, raw materials, or innovations encouraged by industrial policy. Can there be a similar developmental strategy based upon the service sector? Indeed, can the Indian IT sector advance beyond provision of call centers and back-office services to production of innovative software? Anecdotal evidence suggests that on the whole, it has not gone far in this direction.

FIGURE 4.2

## Service sector as a share of total exports (1980–2005)

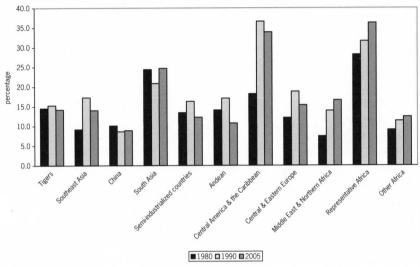

*Source*: UNCTAD (2007).

Aside from service activities associated with information and communications technologies, there has also been a boom of other types of services. Tourism, an expanding service activity worldwide, has been dynamic in many developing countries. Again, to what extent do these services serve as a source of linkages and productivity growth? Banking, insurance, and business consulting services have also boomed but have remained highly concentrated in industrial countries.

Looking at the trends in the overall trade in services is one way to begin to address these questions. Figure 4.2 shows that service exports have been modest. As a share of total exports of goods and services, the latter fluctuate between 9 percent and 16 percent for most regions, with China as the lowest. At the other end of the scale, South Asia, Central America and the Caribbean, and Representative Africa had service exports amounting to between 25 percent and 36 percent of the total exports.

Comparing figure 4.2 with exports of services by types of activities in table 4.2 shows that the Central American and Caribbean and the Representative Africa regions (mainly Kenya in the latter) had high contributions from tourism, which develops some linkages (demand for foodstuffs and some basic manufactures) but typically does not lead to significant technological learning.

TABLE 4.2

## Breakdown of Regions' Exports of Services

| | % of total exports of services | | | | | |
|---|---|---|---|---|---|---|
| Region | 1980 | 1985 | 1990 | 1995 | 2000 | 2005 |
| Tigers | | | | | | |
| Transportation | 39 | 34 | 25 | 33 | 35 | 36 |
| Travel | 25 | 30 | 36 | 27 | 22 | 18 |
| Other services | 36 | 37 | 39 | 40 | 43 | 46 |
| Southeast Asia[a] | | | | | | |
| Transportation | 16 | 14 | 14 | 9 | 17 | 22 |
| Travel | 40 | 43 | 57 | 49 | 65 | 44 |
| Other services | 44 | 43 | 29 | 42 | 18 | 34 |
| China[b] | | | | | | |
| Transportation | 52 | 43 | 46 | 18 | 12 | 21 |
| Travel | 28 | 32 | 30 | 46 | 53 | 39 |
| Other services | 20 | 25 | 24 | 37 | 35 | 40 |
| South Asia[c] | | | | | | |
| Transportation | 20 | 21 | 27 | 31 | 17 | 16 |
| Travel | 45 | 25 | 27 | 29 | 19 | 16 |
| Other services | 36 | 54 | 46 | 40 | 64 | 69 |
| Semi-industrialized countries | | | | | | |
| Transportation | 27 | 32 | 22 | 22 | 19 | 20 |
| Travel | 43 | 41 | 47 | 41 | 43 | 54 |
| Other services | 30 | 27 | 31 | 37 | 39 | 26 |
| Andean | | | | | | |
| Transportation | 32 | 39 | 40 | 36 | 22 | 25 |
| Travel | 39 | 30 | 31 | 36 | 50 | 53 |
| Other services | 28 | 31 | 28 | 28 | 27 | 21 |
| Central America & the Caribbean | | | | | | |
| Transportation | 20 | 16 | 13 | 10 | 11 | 12 |
| Travel | 46 | 58 | 57 | 65 | 71 | 72 |
| Other services | 34 | 26 | 30 | 25 | 17 | 16 |
| Central & Eastern Europe[d] | | | | | | |
| Transportation | 51 | 48 | 38 | 23 | 23 | 27 |
| Travel | 20 | 21 | 22 | 35 | 49 | 38 |
| Other services | 29 | 30 | 40 | 42 | 29 | 35 |
| Middle East & Northern Africa[e] | | | | | | |
| Transportation | 25 | — | — | — | — | — |
| Travel | 29 | — | — | — | — | — |
| Other services | 45 | 54 | 53 | 44 | 43 | 40 |

(continued)

**TABLE 4.2**  *(continued)*

| | % of total exports of services | | | | | |
| --- | --- | --- | --- | --- | --- | --- |
| Region | 1980 | 1985 | 1990 | 1995 | 2000 | 2005 |
| Representative Africa[f] | | | | | | |
| Transportation | 28 | 29 | — | 21 | 26 | 24 |
| Travel | 26 | 36 | — | 58 | 50 | 55 |
| Other services | 46 | 35 | 37 | 22 | 25 | 22 |
| Other Africa[g] | | | | | | |
| Transportation | 66 | 50 | 28 | 24 | 17 | 14 |
| Travel | 10 | 10 | 8 | 8 | 9 | 6 |
| Other services | 24 | 39 | 64 | 68 | 75 | 80 |

*Source:* UNCTAD (2007).
[a]1981 as starting year, [b]1982 as starting year, 2003 as end year, [c]2003 as end year, [d]1982 as start year, 2005 without Slovakia, [e]2004 as end year, [f]1981 as starting year, and 1991 instead of 1990, [g]2003 as last year, Cameroon, Cote d'Ivoire and Mozambique

In some cases, when most of the goods used to cater to travelers are imported, not even these linkages are present and tourism resembles assembly manufacturing in its low contribution to domestic value-added.

In contrast to these two regions, South Asia (basically India) recorded an increase in the share of its services other than travel and transportation. Table 4.3 adds one more piece of information: the rise of service sector share in exports in South Asia is mostly attributable to expansion of "dynamic" service exports associated with information and communications technologies. Such exports are dynamic in the sense that they generate high value-added and utilize skilled labor as compared to travel and transportation services. Indian experience suggests, in particular, that specialization in services with higher value-added can help growth and income per capita. Nevertheless, an overwhelming 93 percent of India's labor force remains unemployed or underemployed in the agricultural and urban informal sectors.

Elsewhere, the connection between exports of services and economic growth appears to be mixed. The fast-growing countries, such as the Tigers and China, have consistently seen an expansion of exports in "other services," mainly banking, insurance, and business services. Other services have also been increasing and make up 35 percent of total service exports in Central and Eastern Europe, with business-related activities taking the dominant share. This increase in other services is also true of some semi-industrialized countries—e.g., Brazil. However, given the low share of service exports in general in these economies, it is hard to argue that they have played an important role in their growth processes.

TABLE 4.3

## Exports of Information and Communications Services as a Percentage of Total Service Exports

| Region | Share in service exports |
| --- | --- |
| Tigers | 0.8 |
| Southeast Asia | 0.6 |
| China | 2.5 |
| South Asia[a] | 39.8 |
| Semi-industrialized countries | 1.2 |
| Andean | 0.0 |
| Central America & the Caribbean[b] | 2.5 |
| Central & Eastern Europe | 2.3 |
| Middle East & Northern Africa | 0.5 |
| Representative Africa | 1.0 |
| Other Africa[a] | 0.3 |

*Source:* UNCTAD (2007).
[a]2003
[b]2004

## Terms of Trade

Failing to diversify exports toward products with higher domestic value-added and technological content always carries risks of adverse terms of trade movements that affect primary commodities but increasingly also low-tech manufactures, which are associated with low-demand elasticities and low wages in producing countries.[2] Such adverse shocks result, in turn, in declines in export revenues and potential foreign exchange bottlenecks. Even favorable terms-of-trade shifts can set off Dutch disease and similar afflictions in primary goods exporters.

As discussed in chapter 2, the economic slowdown in most developing countries that started in the second half of the 1970s and deepened during the lost decade of the 1980s was partially associated with falling terms of trade for nonmanufactured products. Terms of trade for commodities fell by around 30 percent from the average of the first three-and-a-half decades following World War II. The collapse lasted about a quarter century. As export values plummeted, many economies went into recession or an outright growth collapse. The slowdown was worsened by a sudden cutoff in net financial transfers to the developing countries at the beginning of 1980s (especially in Latin America).

The downward trend in prices for primary commodities that began in the 1970s was not something new. Decades previously, in the late 1940s, two structuralist economists, Raúl Prebisch (1950) and Hans Singer (1950), put forth a theory on the effects of declining terms of trade for developing economies. They maintained that as economies around the world grow richer, the structure of their demand changes toward manufacturing products (and now, more recently, dynamic services). The use of synthetics to replace raw materials in the production of manufactured goods will bring about a further decline in the relative demand for primary commodities. Terms of trade will thereby move unfavorably, leading to declining net export values and adverse effects on growth.

Figure 4.3, updated from Ocampo and Parra (2003), confirms this view. The figure presents the long-run trend of real prices for nonfuel primary commodities throughout the twentieth and early twenty-first centuries.[3] Commodity prices are compared with the manufacturing unit value index developed by the United Nations and now regularly updated by the World Bank. Thus, the trends describe how prices of primary commodities fared relative to manufacturing products for the last century or so. Despite upward spikes early in the last century and in the 1920s, 1950s, and 1970s, the overall downward trend is quite clear. For the twentieth century as a whole, raw materials recorded a decline of more than 50 percent in their value relative to manufactures. Among different commodities, tropical agricultural products fared the worst, while metals did somewhat better (not shown in figure 4.3).

**FIGURE 4.3**

**Ratio of aggregate non-oil commodity prices to manufacturing prices (1900–2005)**

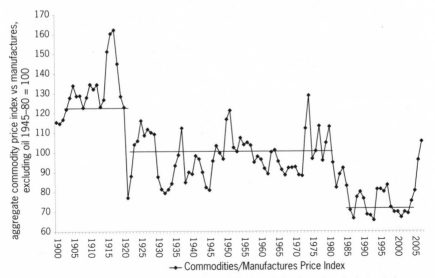

*Sources*: Grilli and Yang (1998), Ocampo and Parra (2003), and update based on the latter study.

Another spike emerged in recent years, together with a boom in oil and other prices (as in the 1970s). These price hikes were propelled in part by the large increase in the demand for raw materials coming from the rapidly growing Chinese economy. Many low-income primary product exporters (not to mention generously endowed Russia and the Persian Gulf countries, among others) saw handsome gains in the terms of trade and grew at relatively decent rates. Unfortunately, this boom came to an end in mid-2008, an event that is likely to curtail economic expansion in much of the developing world.

The solution for ensuring long-term sustainable growth depends on developing countries' ability to diversify their exports toward products with more value-added and technological content. While many economies may not be ready to enter production of high-tech manufacturing, a niche is open for them in other industries where they can still take advantage of increasing returns to scale and avoid risks from unfavorable terms of trade shocks or from a decline in the world demand for primary products.

## Trade Specialization Patterns and Economic Performance

The evidence of a strong association between the patterns of specialization in international trade and economic growth is compelling. Hausmann et al. (2007) use cross-country econometrics to argue that the "quality" or technological content of exports is a basic determinant of growth. These authors measure quality by the income content of exports, estimated as a weighted average of the incomes of countries that typically export the same type of goods. Using a different methodology, Ocampo and Parra (2007) and Ocampo and Vos (2008, chap. 3) come to a similar conclusion.

Table 4.4 uses the latter approach to show the association. We first identify the "dominant" pattern of a specialization—or rather, of the transformation of the export structure—of each country in a given period and then estimate the average per capita growth rates of countries with that specialization pattern. Sanyaja Lall's classification of exports by technological and natural resource contents is again used in table 4.4.

We use two alternative methodologies to determine which specialization pattern is dominant in a specific country and time period. The first method (table 4.4a) is that used by Ocampo and Vos (2008, chap. 3). It is based on the change in the share of a specific export category weighted by a measure of the "revealed comparative advantage" (RCA) of the country in that category of goods at the end of the period (the share of the country in that category of exports in world markets relative to its overall share in world exports).[4] The second method (table 4.4b) also determines the change in the share of the specific export category multiplied by a dummy that indicates whether the country has a "revealed comparative advantage" in that category of exports.[5] In both cases, the export category with the highest value of the estimated coefficient of specialization is taken as the "dominant" one during the period.

Table 4.4 presents the averages of per capita GDP growth of each group of countries with similar "dominant" specialization patterns. Estimates are done by decade since the 1970s and two longer subperiods. According to data availability, we include 93 countries in the analysis for 1970–2000 and 67 for periods ending in 2005–2006.

These exercises point to three main conclusions. The first is that growth is closely associated with the technological and natural resource content of exports. Countries with an export pattern dominated by high-tech grow the fastest over the long run, followed by exporters of either mid-tech or low-tech products. In contrast, exporters of natural resource–based manufactures and, in particular, primary products consistently show the worst performance. Both methodologies confirm this conclusion, with the second accentuating the advantage of high-tech exports.

The second main conclusion is that high-tech and low-tech manufactures offer more stable growth patterns, while the other three categories (mid-tech and the two natural resource–based categories) are subject to stronger cyclical swings, largely associated with fluctuations in commodity prices. Growth in countries with these export patterns has been rapid when commodity prices have been good (the 1970s and the 2000s) and weak or negative when commodity prices have been poor (the 1980s in particular). This association of mid-tech exporters with commodity prices no doubt reflects the importance of the process industries included in that category, which may be seen as having increasing commodity characteristics.

The specific advantage of low-tech over mid-tech specialization patterns is clearly associated with greater stability of growth; during periods of high commodity prices mid-tech exporters actually grow faster. On the other hand, the advantage of mid- over low-tech specialization is obviously technological. So, there is a trade-off between these two features, with the technological factor prevailing in 1990–2006 but not in the 1980–2006 period as a whole. In turn, although mid-tech exporters are also cyclically vulnerable, this specialization pattern is in the long run clearly superior to that based on natural resources (either manufactures or primary goods).

The third main conclusion is that growth, as a corollary of the previous patterns, tends to be more uniform in the developing world during periods of high commodity prices, such as the 1970s and the 2000s, though continued specialization in primary goods seems to be a disadvantage even in those decades, according to most simulations. In the more recent period, as we have seen, a major channel has been the linkages with commodity exporting developing countries generated by Chinese growth. The expectation that a natural resource–based specialization pattern will lead to fast and uniform growth in

**TABLE 4.4**

# Average per Capita GDP Growth per Group According to Alternative Indexes of Dominant Pattern of Specialization

## (A) According to the Trade Specialization Indicator (TSI)

| Specialization pattern according to index T | | 1970–1980 | 1980–1990 | 1990–2000 | 2000–2006 | 1980–2006 | 1990–2006 |
|---|---|---|---|---|---|---|---|
| High-tech manufactures | (5) | 2.7 | 1.33 | 3.15 | 2.85 | 3.33 | 2.59 |
| Medium-tech manufactures | (4) | 3.36 | -1.36 | 2.06 | 3.25 | 1.22 | 2.48 |
| Low-tech manufactures | (3) | 2.5 | 0.85 | 2.06 | 2.05 | 1.3 | 2.04 |
| Natural resources–based manufactures | (2) | 1.82 | -1.05 | 0.65 | 2.71 | 1.13 | 1.92 |
| Primary commodities | (1) | -0.36 | -0.53 | 0.59 | 2.07 | 0.88 | 1.45 |
| No dominant pattern | (0) | 0.77 | -0.14 | 0.56 | 1.11 | 0.07 | -0.4 |
| Number of countries | | 92 | 93 | 80 | 67 | 67 | 67 |
| Number of countries with dominant pattern | | 89 | 87 | 73 | 58 | 56 | 63 |

## (B) According to the Revealed Trade Specialization Indicator (RTSI)

| Specialization pattern according to index R | | 1970–1980 | 1980–1990 | 1990–2000 | 2000–2006 | 1980–2006 | 1990–2006 |
|---|---|---|---|---|---|---|---|
| High-tech manufactures | (5) | 3.81 | 3.99 | 2.80 | 4.81 | 3.72 | 3.70 |
| Medium-tech manufactures | (4) | 3.74 | -2.33 | 1.33 | 3.07 | 0.61 | 2.68 |
| Low-tech manufactures | (3) | 2.45 | 1.83 | 2.07 | 2.05 | 1.34 | 1.98 |
| Natural resources–based manufactures | (2) | 1.74 | -0.84 | 0.53 | 2.14 | 0.81 | 1.97 |
| Primary commodities | (1) | -0.39 | -0.63 | 0.04 | 2.60 | 0.80 | 1.54 |
| Highest lost share in 1 | | 2.15 | 0.10 | 1.14 | 0.39 | 1.10 | 0.54 |
| Highest lost share in 2 | | 2.29 | -0.37 | 0.16 | -0.01 | 0.50 | -0.11 |
| Highest lost share in 3, 4, or 5 | | 2.81 | | 9.31 | 2.75 | | 3.08 |
| Number of countries | | 91 | 92 | 92 | 66 | 66 | 66 |
| Number of countries with only negative change | | 26 | 17 | 15 | 12 | 7 | 10 |
| Number of countries without data | | 1 | 0 | 0 | 26 | 26 | 26 |

the developing world is thus dependent on commodity prices remaining strong—an expectation unfortunately ungrounded in history.

## A Primer on the Policy Implications

The major policy implications of these empirical findings have already been sketched in chapter 1, and the details are presented in the following chapters.

The high points are that sustained per capita income growth is impossible without productivity increases in at least some activities producing traded goods. As emphasized in chapter 1, industrial and trade interventions have to be designed to support the transformation of the production and trade structures and, particularly, to promote production processes subject to increasing returns. The international policy environment under the fading Washington consensus and the supervision of the World Bank and the World Trade Organization is less favorable to an aggressive policy approach than it was a few decades ago, but many possibilities still exist (see chapters 8 and 9).

In the shorter term macroeconomic dynamics, the management of shocks coming from trade is essential to guarantee stable growth over time under all specialization patterns, but particularly in those patterns that are subject to strong terms-of-trade shocks. The crucial links come through the current account, which can change dramatically and unexpectedly at any time. In a country with a small population, incapable of producing capital and many essential intermediate goods, the overriding macroeconomic restriction during crises is "external strangulation," in the sense of having low hard currency inflows from exports or capital inflows. Gap models as discussed in chapter 7 provide a framework for analyzing the problem but are not a solution. Creating new sources of foreign exchange is basically the only way out.

At the other extreme, ample access to foreign exchange can cause its own problems—overvaluation, slow or aborted industrialization, Dutch disease, and unsustainable economic expansion. The emphasis in this chapter has been on impacts of price spikes for raw material exports, but potential problems go well beyond those posed by bonanzas. The root of the English "bonanza" is an old Spanish word for fair weather, which always comes to an end.

## Notes

1. Data from *World Trade Organization Statistics Database* (see World Trade Organization's Statistics database, covering merchandise trade by commodity from 1980 to 2008, available at: http://stat.wto.org/Home/WSDBHome.aspx?Language=E) show that the mining sector gained a significant share in imports, from 5 percent in 1980 to 13 percent by 2003, as a result of the energy supplies that China obtains abroad, while mining exports declined from 27 percent to 4 percent, respectively, for the same period.

2. High-tech manufactures experiencing rapid technical change (e.g., computer chips) may also experience a fall in the terms of trade, but this phenomenon is different from that experienced by resource-based goods and low-tech manufactures, where low-demand elasticities and cost factors not associated with productivity (low wages, in particular) play the leading role. A more similar issue to that underscored in the main text is that of mid- or high-tech manufactures with blueprints that can be easily transferable and become subject to integrated production systems (e.g., computer assembly).

3. The indices that enter this figure were originally developed by Grilli and Yang (1988) for the period 1900–1986.

4. Formally, this index (T) is: $T_{(\beta, \alpha, k-k+1)} = (CS_{\beta, \alpha, k+1} - CS_{\beta, \alpha, k}) * (TS_{\beta, \alpha, k+1})$, where $CS_{\beta, \alpha, k}$ is the share of category $\alpha$ in total merchandise exports of country $\beta$ in period $k$; and $TS_{\alpha, k+1}$ is the share of country $\beta$'s exports of category $\alpha$ in developing countries' exports of category $\alpha$ in period $k+1$. If we divide the second term by the country's share in world exports, we would have the commonly used measure of revealed comparative advantage in that category, but since this term is common to all categories we exclude it from the equation.

5. Again, formally, $R_{(\beta, \alpha, k-k+1)} = (CS_{\beta, \alpha, k+1} - CS_{\beta, \alpha, k}) * (DRCA_{\beta, \alpha, k+1})$, where $DRCA_{\beta, \alpha, k+1} = 1$ if $RCA_{\beta, \alpha, k+1} > 1$ and 0 otherwise. This measure allows the identification of cases in which the dominant change in pattern was to move away from a sector in which a country had previously reached RCA, even if the country had not reached RCA in any new sector. That is shown in table 4.4 as countries with only negative changes in $CS_{\beta, \alpha}$, classified according to the sector in which they had the strongest loss in share.

# CHAPTER 5

# Patterns of Net Borrowing in Open Developing Economies

THIS SHORT AND FINAL empirical chapter looks at net-lending flows—incomes minus expenditures—over time for the government, private, and rest of the world normalized in all cases by GDP. Long debates and many policy recommendations have followed from the interpretation of how net lending by different sectors relate to each other. We therefore review the conceptual debate first. This review also serves as an introduction to the short-term macroeconomic analysis of chapter 7.

As an accounting identity, of course, total net borrowings must sum to zero:

$$\text{(Private Investment} - \text{Savings)} + \text{(Public Spending} - \text{Taxes)} + \text{(Exports} - \text{Imports)} = 0,$$

with a positive entry indicating that a sector is a net contributor to effective demand. An alternative way to present this identity is by expressing it in terms of deficits (with a positive magnitude indicating that there is a deficit and, therefore, a net borrowing requirement), with the external deficit (negative current account balance) placed at the right-hand side of the identity:

$$\text{Private Sector Deficit} + \text{Fiscal Deficit} = \text{External Deficit.}$$

Since the external deficit has to be financed, this identity can also be expressed as

$$\text{Private Sector Deficit} + \text{Fiscal Deficit} = \text{Net External Financing.}$$

A favorite topic in the macroeconomic literature has been to identify possible "twins," that is, parallel movements of the external deficit and domestic deficits on the left-hand side of the equation, as well as opposite movements of private and fiscal deficits ("crowding out"), to guarantee that overall net borrowings add up to zero.

In the orthodox literature on developing countries, the most commonly emphasized twins are the co-movements of fiscal and current account deficits.

As we will see, this phenomenon has occurred sporadically at most, indicating that the widely accepted "twin deficits" view of macro adjustment does not seem to apply.

An alternative twin, private/foreign, is actually more common, implying that current account deficits largely reflect pro-cyclical swings in *private* spending that are financed by borrowing from the rest of the world. These twin private/external deficits are, of course, common during booms, when there is easy access to foreign capital, but are reduced or turned into surpluses during crises, when external financing dries out. This pattern indicates, furthermore, that there is no "consumption-smoothing" behavior—an important feature of mainstream "Ricardian equivalence" analysis.

Whereas the most commonly emphasized twins do not seem to provide a good description of how developing economies perform, macroeconomic flexibility may be crucial. Particularly, it is important that the macroeconomy be able to absorb strong fluctuations in external financing and associated private deficits/surpluses. Such fluctuations did not derail growth in the Tigers and Southeast Asia in the 1980s. In turn, China, India, and some Tigers continued to grow through the turbulent late 1990s. But other countries and regions have been unable to manage such swings in capital flows. These ideas are developed further in chapter 7.

## Traditional Interpretations

At least four incompatible contemporary doctrines propose explanations of how open macroeconomies operate. As previously indicated, twin fiscal/external deficits (TD) and Ricardian equivalence (RE) dogmata are widely spread in mainstream literature. In contrast, development and heterodox economists often favor structural gap (SG) and unstable external financing (UEF) explanations of macroeconomic balances in developing countries.

In development macroeconomics, the twin-deficits hypothesis traces back at least to the IMF economist Jacques Polak's (1957) blueprint for the "financial programming" exercises, which to this day are the linchpin of the International Monetary Fund's stabilization packages. The recipe for action is to cut the fiscal deficit, which is supposed to improve the economy's external position. Polak was drawing on a long tradition of monetarist analysis of the balance of payments. In one variant, unless the private sector chooses to increase its saving—or, more precisely, reduce its net borrowing—a higher fiscal deficit must be paid for by domestic money creation.[1] Aggregate demand consequently goes up. Under tacit assumptions that all resources are fully employed and the domestic price level is tied to foreign prices by arbitrage in foreign trade (purchasing power parity, or PPP, applies), the higher demand has to spill over into a larger external deficit.

Ricardian equivalence (Barro 1974) emerges from dynamic optimal savings models postulating that all resources are fully employed and that households smooth their consumption (or, more generally, expenditure including residential investment) over time. It plays a far more central role in contemporary mainstream macroeconomics than Polak's somewhat dated monetarism. Along the lines of Say's Law, RE broadly asserts that a change in fiscal net borrowing will be offset by an equal shift in private net lending. In this context, traditional counter-cyclical fiscal policy cannot play any role, as it would be counterbalanced by an opposing response from the private sector. For example, as fiscal deficits increase, the private sector saves more in anticipation of the taxes that it will have to pay in the future to defray the additional public sector debt. In an open economy context, any one country's external position will then be determined by intertemporal trade-offs between consumption and saving with all countries in the world producing the same good (Obstfeld and Rogoff 1997).[2]

TD and RE stories are not compatible because they assign different roles to private net borrowing and net external financing. Under TD, private borrowing is "neutral" in that it does not respond to shifts in the external or fiscal positions. Under RE, the current account (net external financing) is neutral with regard to fiscal shifts while private and government borrowing dance the trade-offs.

It must be emphasized that, even if the negative correlations predicted by the TD and RE frameworks hold, their assumptions about macroeconomic causality may not be valid. Causality can be interpreted as running the other way—from the external to the fiscal and/or private sector financial gap, or from private to public, respectively. Particularly, if as discussed in chapter 1, the economy is externally constrained, the external position may be "structural," according to a SG framework, and will therefore persist in the face of plausible domestic policy changes. This persistence means that, within "reasonable" ranges of real exchange rate values and the level of economic activity, the trade deficit—or surplus, say, for China or Japan—will not change by very much. The economy can also be externally constrained during periods of scarce external financing, as the UEF hypothesis would predict, generating the same type of problems during cyclical downswings.

Similarly, causality may run counter to the assumptions of the RE hypothesis. In traditional Keynesian analysis, for example, swings in private deficits run the show, either through autonomous variations of investment ("animal spirits") or in the propensity to consume. Counter-cyclical fiscal policy is called for to compensate for the swings in the associated private sector balances. If private spending is weak, generating low investment or consumption (high private net lending), a fiscal deficit comes forth to absorb the private surplus (and a fiscal surplus, if private net borrowing is exuberant). If high private lending is not offset by fiscal borrowing, a recession would ensue, reducing tax revenues that would generate a fiscal deficit anyway. These reactions reproduce the off-setting private and fiscal deficits of the RE story but with reverse causality.

## Structuralist Interpretations

SG analysis resembles full-employment RE in that a binding external gap imposes a supply constraint on the system. Particularly, in a developing country context, the question becomes: how does effective demand adjust to meet the supply constraints imposed by available imports? To hold demand stable, any shift in the private or public sector net-borrowing position has to be reflected into an offsetting change in the other domestic gap. So, if fiscal policy is targeted to expand economic activity by increasing public sector spending, it would generate inflationary pressures. Inflation tax and forced saving mechanisms would then kick in, reducing real demand by the private sector—that is, a private sector surplus is forcefully generated to finance the fiscal deficit (Taylor 2004). The process can also work in reverse. If we focus on variations in external financing, and private net borrowing is assumed to be neutral, then fiscal deficits will be determined by shifts in the external gap: TD with causality reversed.

This dynamic behavior has been highlighted in the UEF literature, although it focuses on domestic private rather than (or at least as much as) on fiscal balances (see, for example, Stiglitz et al. 2006, part 3; Ffrench-Davis 2006, 2008; Ocampo 2008). This literature emphasizes the fact that private capital flows to the developing world—more to the middle-income or "emerging economies" than to the poorest ones—are unstable. Three strong financing cycles have been experienced since the 1970s: abundance in the second half of the 1970s, largely due to the recycling of oil surpluses, followed by extreme scarcity during the "lost decade" of the 1980s; abundance again beginning in the early 1990s, followed by renewed scarcity in the aftermath of the Asian and Russian crises of 1997 and 1998, respectively; and abundance again since 2004, followed by more moderate flows after the U.S. subprime crisis of mid-2007 and a freeze in financing following the world financial meltdown of September 2008.

Domestic balances adjust to the availability of external financing, along lines similar to those emphasized in the SG literature. In the 1970s, many governments borrowed heavily, so fiscal deficits were the counterpart of abundant external financing. The pattern was a twin fiscal/external deficit, but with the causality reversed in relation to the Polak framework. For countries of the Southern Cone of Latin America, private rather than fiscal deficits were then the counterpart (or twin) of the "exuberance" in external financing. Both sorts of responses were led by liberalization of the domestic financial sector and the capital account, and eventually led to massive private bankruptcies and domestic financial crises (and associated public sector rescues) when capital stopped flowing in. Later on, crises driven from abroad became the pattern in the developing world. Referring to the Mexican "Tequila" crisis of 1994, IMF Managing Director Michel Camdessus called the associated meltdown "the first crisis of the twentieth-first century." However, events of this type had been inaugurated in modern times by the Southern Cone countries (particularly Chile) in the early 1980s, and there were many precedents further in the past (recall the 1930s, for example). All these crises were not so much a "twenty-first" century pattern of fast reaction from the financial markets but rather a consequence of structural features of economies subject to strong cyclical swings in external financing.

## What Does the Data Say?

It becomes interesting to see what patterns emerge from the data. Table 5.1 presents partial correlation coefficients among the three possible pairs of balances. The strongest message that emerges is that the private/external twin is much more common (nine out of the 12 regions) than the traditional Polak public/external twin. Only five regions show the statistically significant negative coefficient predicted by the TD story, but in three of them the alternative twin seems more powerful; in a fourth one, North Africa and the Middle East, the coefficient, although significant, is rather small. This finding makes the TD

**TABLE 5.1**

## Correlation Coefficients for Institutional Sectors' Net-Borrowing Flows

| Region | Period | Government-Foreign | Private-Foreign | Private-Government |
|---|---|---|---|---|
| Tigers | 1981–2006 | −0.48* | −0.96** | 0.21 |
| Southeast Asia | 1979–2006 | 0.25 | −0.92** | −0.61** |
| China | 1982–2006 | 0.47* | −0.96** | −0.71** |
| South Asia | 1979–2006 | −0.47* | −0.78** | −0.19 |
| Semi-industrialized countries | 1980–2006 | −0.07 | −0.73** | −0.63** |
| Andean | 1977–2006 | 0.09 | −0.76** | −0.72** |
| Central America & the Caribbean | 1977–2006 | −0.54** | −0.69** | −0.24 |
| Central & Eastern Europe | 1990–2006 | −0.12 | −0.79** | −0.51* |
| Russia & Ukraine | 1995–2006 | −0.74** | −0.45 | −0.26 |
| Representative Africa | 1980–2006 | −0.20 | −0.32 | −0.87** |
| Other Africa | 1980–2005 | −0.26 | −0.73** | −0.46* |
| Middle East & Northern Africa | 1981–2006 | −0.45* | −0.32 | −0.70** |

*Source:* United Nations (2007c).
*Correlation is significant at 5%
**Correlation is significant at 1%

hypothesis of limited empirical relevance. Indeed, only the former USSR shows a dominant Polak twin, with causality subject to debate (see below). The centrality of shifts in external financing indicates that this variable is far from "neutral," and thus the RE story is largely irrelevant.

The dominance of the private/external twin is evident in the three cases that are shown in detail in figure 5.1. In the Tigers, the fiscal role was rather passive. The private and foreign co-movements were very large, with swings up and down exceeding 10 percent of GDP (figure 5.1a). Maintaining very high per capita income growth over a 25-year period with the macroeconomy subject to such extreme fluctuations is a feat perhaps unprecedented historically. However, some of them stumbled during the Asian crisis, indicating that even the best-performing countries can face difficulties managing external financial volatility.

In five out of the nine cases, there was a mix between a dominant private/external twin and offsetting movements between private and fiscal deficits. In two cases, Southeast Asia and China, these domestic movements clearly reflect counter-cyclical fiscal policy. As the swings in external financing led to parallel movements in private sector balances, public sector finances tried to compensate, a fact that is reflected in the positive correlation between the fiscal balance and external financing. Figure 5.1b illustrates the case of Southeast Asia. In this case, again, the very strong private/external swing is accompanied by counter-cyclical movements of fiscal balances: deficits during the 1980s followed by small surpluses during the booming 1990–1997 period and deficits again during the Asian crisis, gradually corrected thereafter.

The semi-industrialized countries show a case in which a dominant private/external twin is mixed with a negative correlation between private and fiscal deficits, but there are no signs of counter-cyclical fiscal policy (the other two cases are the small Andean countries and Other Africa). Except for the recessionary "lost decade" of the 1980s, this region appears to have a more or less structural external deficit. The wide offsetting swings in net government and private borrowing are associated with the "lost decade," with the interpretation following SG or UEF lines, as the dominant constraint was clearly foreign exchange availability. Despite IMF programs, public sectors faced difficulties balancing the budget. Given foreign exchange constraints, the inflation tax and forced savings kicked in to generate the private sector surplus necessary to "finance" the budget deficit.

As indicated, there are only three regions for which the private/external twin is not dominant. One of them, the former USSR, is the only case in which the Polak twin dominates, although given the relatively short period for which the analysis was run, its empirical relevance remains dubious. The causality also seems to be the opposite of that assumed by the TD literature, as the improvement in the fiscal balance that underlies the story seems to be associated

FIGURE 5.1

## Resource gaps by institutional sectors in (A) Tigers (1976–2006), (B) Southeast Asia (1979–2006), and (C) semi-industrialized countries (1980–2006)

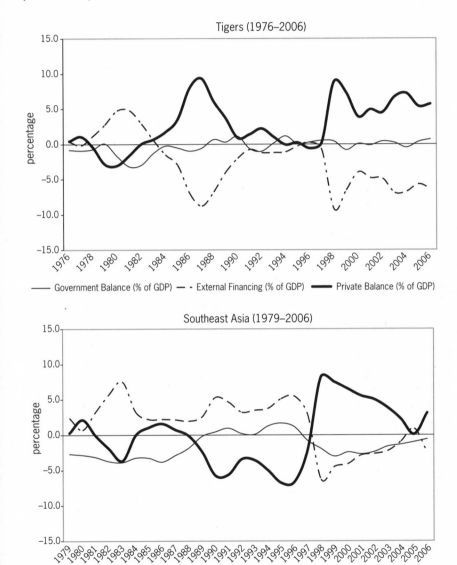

(continued)

Semi-industrialized Countries (1980–2006)

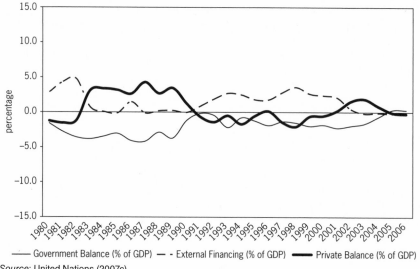

—— Government Balance (% of GDP) — - External Financing (% of GDP) ▬▬ Private Balance (% of GDP)
Source: United Nations (2007c).

**FIGURE 5.2**

## Resource gaps by institutional sectors in (A) Russia and Ukraine (1995–2006) and (B) Representative Africa (1980–2006)

Russia & Ukraine (1995–2006)

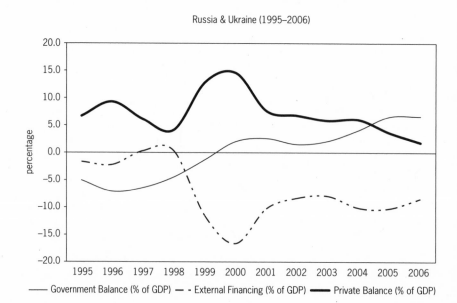

—— Government Balance (% of GDP) — - External Financing (% of GDP) ▬▬ Private Balance (% of GDP)

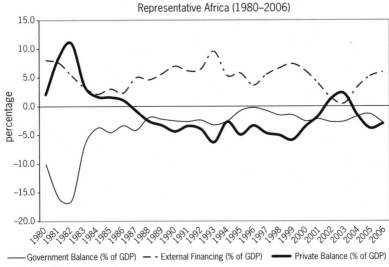

Source: United Nations (2007c).

first with the strong fiscal adjustments that were forced upon Russia by the 1998 crisis, followed in the mid-2000s by the strong fiscal effects of booming oil revenues (figure 5.2a).

Finally, figure 5.2b shows the history of one of the two regions where a strong offsetting behavior of domestic balances was not associated with any dominant external twin, Representative Africa (the other is the Middle East and Northern Africa). The story seems again dominated by events during the "lost decade," and thus by foreign exchange scarcity. Indeed, starting in the 1990s, this region looks much more like one dominated by a private/external twin with fiscal policy playing a rather passive role.

## Notes

1. In terms of chapter 6, the assumption that the fiscal deficit must be paid for by domestic money creation means that the IMF simply disregards the role of a domestic market for government bonds.
2. In the RE view, the bilateral trade deficit of the United States with China would be "explained" by a higher rate of time preference in the former.

## CHAPTER 6

# Financial Structures

THE FINANCIAL SIDE of an economy undergoes structural change through the development process. There is no strict progression of financial development and initial conditions matter. But, broadly speaking, new financial structures gradually evolve, in a process that can be seen as a sequence of five "stages" of increasing financial complexity. Understanding financial structures is crucial for the analysis of macroeconomic policy in chapter 7, since they can increase policy flexibility but can also constrain policy maneuver and generate risks of destabilization for the entire macroeconomy.

## National Financial Accounts

The underlying concepts are a blend of flows of funds accounting and more traditional approaches. The main distinction lies in the treatment of "equity" or "net worth." When consolidated economy-wide, the net worth of the business sector has to be the value of its assets less liabilities. According to the flows of funds, the liabilities include debt *plus* the market value of the sector's outstanding shares. A more conventional alternative is to define "equity" as the value of assets minus debt. In the late 1990s in the United States during the stock market boom, business net worth was negative by the former definition and equal to zero (as it always is) by the latter. Net worth in the U.S. flows of funds was positive as of mid-2008.

Table 6.1 defines the balance sheets for six types of agents, or sectors: private non-financial actors, the government, the central bank, commercial banks, a non-bank financial sector, and the rest of the world.[1] The entries represent values of *stocks* of financial claims. Many financial instruments are included in the table. We begin by considering a very restricted subset of them and then bring more claims into play in successive stages of finance.

**TABLE 6.1**

## Illustrative Balance Sheets ("T-accounts")

| Private | | Commercial banks | | Finance | | Central bank | | Government | | Rest of the world | |
|---|---|---|---|---|---|---|---|---|---|---|---|
| $P_K K$ | $L_P$ | $L$ | $H$ | $P_V V_F$ | $L_F$ | $B_{cent}$ | $\eta$ | $\Gamma$ | $B$ | $eL^*$ | $eR^*$ |
| $H_P$ | $eL_P^*$ | $B_{comm}$ | $\Phi$ | $QS_F$ | $eL_F^*$ | $eR^*$ | $A$ | | $eL_G^*$ | $P_V V^*$ | $e\Omega^*$ |
| $B_P$ | $P_V V$ | $\eta$ | $QS$ | $Z$ | $Z$ | $\Phi$ | | | | $B^*$ | |
| $A_P$ | $M_P$ | $A_{comm}$ | $\Omega_{comm}$ | | $\Omega_F$ | | | | | | |
| $P_C C$ | $\Omega_P$ | $M$ | | | | | | | | | |
| $\Omega_{comm}$ | | | | | | | | | | | |
| $\Omega_F$ | | | | | | | | | | | |

Total wealth: $P_K K + P_C C + \Gamma = \Omega_P + e\Omega_R^*$
Net foreign assets: $-e\Omega^* = e(R^* - L_P^* - L_G^* - L_F^*) - P_V V^* - B^*$
Bank loan balance: $L_P + L_F - L = 0$
Government bond balance: $B_P + B_{comm} + B_{cent} + B^* - B = 0$
Central bank bond balance: $A_P + A_{comm} - A = 0$
Foreign loan balance: $e(L_P^* + L_G^*) - eL^* = 0$
Equity balance: $P_V(V_F + V^*) - P_V V = 0$
Mortgage balance: $MP - M - 0$
*Note:* Finance refers to financial institutions excluding commercial banks.

Values of claims can change in two ways. One is through *flow* accumulation or decumulation over time of the stocks in response to net lending or borrowing by different actors. The other mechanism applies to outstanding shares and foreign loans that have explicit asset prices (a price index for equity and the exchange rate, respectively), so their values can jump "instantaneously" due to capital gains or losses.

## Stage I Finance

The simplest financial structure, which we will call Stage I, still applies in a large number of developing countries today. In normal times (one historically significant sort of "abnormality" is considered later in this chapter), the only private assets are "money" (broadly construed), $H_p$, and the value of tangible capital, $P_K K$, with $K$ as the existing stock at historical or replacement cost and $P_K$ as its asset price.

On the liability side, private business and households may borrow $L_p$ from the banks, but loans from abroad, $eL_p^*$, and the value of equity outstanding, $P_V V$, are negligible or effectively nontraded. There is no significant market in bonds, so private $(B_p)$ and commercial bank $(B_{comm})$ holdings of government securities are near zero. The government's total borrowing, which at this stage is only from the central bank, is $B=B_{cent}$. The corresponding asset is the "full faith and credit" of the state, $\Gamma$.

The money supply, $H$, is the sole liability of the commercial banking system.[2] In simple financial systems, a typical monetary policy instrument is to require commercial banks to hold reserves (or "high-powered money"), $\eta$, against deposits, according to a rule such as $\eta=\rho H$ with $\rho<1$ (assuming for simplicity that all money is held as deposits in the banking system).[3]

Besides deposit reserves, the only commercial bank asset is outstanding credit or loans, $L$ (at this stage only $L_p$ to the private sector). The banks' balance sheet is $L+\eta=H$, implying that $L$ and $H$ are linked via the reserve requirement. Boosting $\rho$ forces banks to contract both money and credit. For reasons discussed later in this chapter, in more sophisticated systems reserve ratios tend to be minimal and other regulatory methods are used.

Besides the bonds, $B_{cent}$, placed with it in one way or another by the government, the central bank's only other asset is international reserves, $eR^*$, with $R^*$ as the value of reserves in foreign currency and $e$ as the exchange rate (units of local currency per unit of foreign currency). Consolidating the accounts of the central and commercial banks shows that the money supply is given by the equation $H=L+B_{cent}+eR^*$, so that it is equal to total domestic credit plus foreign reserves. As will be seen in the following sections, formulas of this sort play a central role in monetarist macroeconomics in general and its particular incarnation in the form of IMF financial programming.

Liquidity is often interpreted as a measure of the financial flexibility of an individual actor, group of actors, or the financial system as a whole. It constitutes "wherewithal"—the resources readily available for purposes of capital formation or financial transactions. For the private sector in Stage I, liquidity takes the form of one asset, namely money. Nothing else is at hand.

The accounting framework just sketched puts strict limitations on policy options. First, it is the preferred arena for the IMF's venerable version of open economy monetarism. Suppose that money demand is described by the equation of exchange $H_pV=PX$, with $P$ as the price level, $X$ as output, and $V$ as an institutionally determined "velocity" of circulation of money, which in the most simple frameworks is assumed to be constant. If $X$ is set by "full employment" and $P$ comes from an inflation forecast or target, then money demand must follow.

Suppose, somewhat mysteriously, that money demand is always equal to supply, $H_p=H$. If loans, $L_p$, to the private sector are set by needs of production, the sum of bank loans to the government and international reserves is determined from the consolidated banking system's balance sheet: $B_{cent}+eR^*=H-L_p$. If international reserves are targeted to increase as the current account or inflow of external finance improves, then government debt, $B=B_{cent}$, must fall via a larger fiscal surplus. This exercise is the basis for the "twin" fiscal/foreign deficits that are at the heart of IMF financial programming.

Along with twin deficit hawks worldwide, the IMF implicitly assumes that causality runs from the fiscal to foreign deficit. But as we saw in chapter 5, it can easily go the other way. Furthermore, as we pointed out in that chapter, these particular twins are not frequently observed in the data. Roughly parallel movements of external financing and private net-borrowing flows are a more frequent phenomenon.

Stage I accounts also support the basic closed economy monetarist inflation model, set out by the Swedish economist Knut Wicksell in the late nineteenth century and propagandized worldwide by Milton Friedman and disciples as recently as the 1970s and 1980s. The logic is that a higher fiscal deficit gets "monetized" (because the government cannot place debt obligations except with the central bank). Still on the assumptions that money demand equals supply, and that economic activity ($X$) is constantly at full employment, the resulting increase in $H_p=H$ forces $P$ to go up, as determined by the equation of exchange written in the form $P=H_pV/X$.

Because liquidity in many economies now comprises a spectrum of financial assets and liabilities far wider than simple money, financial programming and monetarist inflation models are often anachronistic. Inflation in Zimbabwe, which took off in the mid-2000s, can be interpreted along monetarist lines, but this phenomenon is not common today.

Finally, it is worth noting that even in simple Stage I finance (and certainly in the more complicated systems discussed in following sections), financial manias can appear in "abnormal" circumstances. Unfortunately, such situations have arisen pretty regularly for the last 400 years.[4]

One familiar scenario is based on government assets, $P_GG$ (with an asset price, $P_G$), that have been privatized and sold through a dealer to the public.[5] If the dealer happens to have a captive bank at his disposal, he can lend money to himself and cronies to bid up the share price leading to a capital gain (or ongoing inflation) at rate $\pi$: the asset price rises to $(1+\pi)P_G$. Other actors may then start borrowing from the captive and other banks to try to buy shares, setting off a boom that ends inevitably in a crash.

Premiere examples were the Mississippi and South Sea crises early in the eighteenth century, in which John Law's Banque Générale in Paris and the Swordblade Bank in London issued the loans. With international complications discussed in following sections, the Chilean crisis of 1982–1983 followed the same pattern around companies privatized by Pinochet's Chicago Boys. These examples illustrate a recurring theme in financial instability: capital gains are financed by liquidity in the form of *liabilities* assumed by financial actors to buy the appreciating assets. Manifold possibilities along these lines are sketched later in the chapter.

## Stage II Finance

The key element in Stage II is a domestic market in (at least short-term) government and/or central bank debt. It may have been created by careful husbandry on the part of the central bank. We first sketch banking system interactions in such a system and then take up broader issues. This discussion brings many more entries in table 6.1 into action.

The conventional treatment of Stage II is to assume that government bonds are held by both the private sector and banks, $B_p + B_{comm} + B_{cent} = B$. In outline form, Keynes in the 1930s thought in terms of this sort of finance, with the significant extension of having markets in corporate debt instruments as well.

In developing countries today, the central bank will often offer in the market its own bonds, $A$, which constitute a non-monetary liability of the institution and may be held by the public and commercial banks, $A_p + A_{comm} = A$. A major advantage of this practice is that it is easier to develop a market for central bank bonds than a fully fledged set of transactions for government (not to mention corporate) paper. The central bank may also provide commercial banks with direct lending or advances, $\Phi$ (from a rediscount window or by injecting funds directly into interbank overnight credit markets), which commercial banks can then use to increase their own loans, $L$, and thereby money, $H$. Finally, we should consider commercial bank own funds or equity, $\Omega_{comm}$, held by the private sector as an asset.

Four monetary policy instruments can be illustrated with table 6.1.

As noted for Stage I, shifting the reserve requirement, $\rho$, is a traditional control mechanism. As discussed in the following sections, this simple tool can be used in attempts to "sterilize" or offset credit and money expansion resulting from increases in international reserves, $eR^*$. But deposit reserve requirements usually generate a strong opposition from commercial banks because these institutions are forced to hold deposits that they cannot lend and therefore increase the cost of financial intermediation. Other monetary policy tools can also be used.

For example, the central bank can increase or decrease its own lending, $\Phi$, to encourage commercial banks to expand or contract their loan book.

More important, open market operations become feasible when commercial banks or the private sector hold significant amounts of government and/or central bank bonds. Once enough of these instruments are traded in the market, to expand the money supply the central bank can buy bonds from commercial banks by crediting their deposits, $\eta$, of high-powered money. Or it can buy bonds from private agents who then place the funds in the banking system as deposits. With excess reserves on hand, the banks have an incentive to increase $L$ and $H$. A complication is that in a crisis commercial banks may prefer to hold higher quantities of government or central bank bonds rather than lend to the private sector. This sort of "liquidity trap" is unfortunately quite common (and appeared with a vengeance among rich country banks in the late 2008 crisis).

In turn, to contract the money supply, the central bank can sell bonds to the banks or the private sector. The objective is to reduce both the money supply and lending to the private sector by commercial banks ($H$ and $L$, respectively).

Finally, contemporary approaches to regulation such as the internationally accepted standards issued by the Basel Committee on Banking Regulation—widely known as Basel I and II—focus on bank capital, $\Omega_{comm}$. Complications are taken up in the following sections.

Turning to macroeconomics more generally, it remains true that primary liquidity in Stage II is still money. Keynesian ideas about liquidity preference come into play, with the interest rate mediating portfolio choice between more liquid money and less liquid bonds (with government and central bank bonds being more liquid than those of the corporate sector, which are subject to interest rate spreads associated with both liquidity and solvency risks). As far as the private sector is concerned, the liquidity spectrum still spans a collection of assets, with specific holdings responding to returns and costs.

If a corporate bond market exists, it can be of significant support to capital formation. But even without one, Stage II governments can issue bonds to fund national development banks specialized in production-oriented loans. As discussed in chapter 8, such institutions have been very important in developing countries; they played a significant postwar reconstruction role in advanced economies as well.

Finally, Keynes analyzed financial instability in terms of sharp shifts in liquidity preference. Mixed with overborrowing (high leverage), they provide the foundation for Minsky's "financial instability hypothesis" (Minsky 1982). The essential insight is that as the confidence of private agents builds up during the boom, they tend to overborrow—from the banks or in corporate bond markets—to buy real assets subject to capital gains (speculation in financial assets will come in later stages), pay for investment, or even to increase consumption.

Sooner or later the borrowers can end up in very risky positions. Even if they were initially secure in the sense of having enough income to cover investment and interest payments (a hedged position), they can increase borrowing and spending to the point where current revenues become insufficient to pay for investment (speculative position), or even for interest payments (Ponzi finance). This sets the stage for a crisis when the end of the credit boom that sustains the borrowing exposes these positions. There can be a credit squeeze as creditors turn risk averse and move into larger holdings of money or government bonds.

In microeconomic terms, the squeeze can be seen as a case of rationing on the part of creditors in a world with "asymmetric information" (Stiglitz and

Greenwald 2003). When risk perceptions rise, it may be rational for lenders to stop giving credit altogether to those borrowers who are viewed as risky, rather than charge them a larger risk premium that would in fact further increase the risk of lending to them. This pattern is the simplest form of a cycle of "appetite for risk" followed by "flight to quality." More complex versions are discussed later in the chapter.

Although Keynes was certainly aware of possibilities for financial instability involving credit booms and asset bubbles, they do not figure prominently in either the *Treatise on Money* or the *General Theory*. Certainly in the post-1929 world that he was analyzing, the use of liabilities as liquidity to acquire assets (allegedly) subject to capital gains was not an immediate threat.

## Stage III Finance

In Stage III foreign financial capital comes onto the scene. The economy gets access to "hard currency" foreign loans ($eL_p^*$ to the private sector and $eL_G^*$ to the government, expressed in domestic prices). Many countries and regions have gone through such a transition—Austria and Germany around 1930 when bank deposits from foreigners were used to acquire domestic assets leading into the Credit-Anstalt crash and Western Europe when capital markets were liberalized in the 1970s.

This stage may be seen as typical for developing countries today. Before the recent commodity price boom, sub-Saharan African countries had seen little development in their financial structures that would take them beyond Stage II or even Stage I, as they continued to be deprived of access to private external financing. In a growing group of developing countries, however, the importance of bond markets, especially central bank and government bonds, has been on the rise, and over the years, they have fared better in attracting external private finance—even if in an unstable way. These countries may be said to be firmly based in Stage III financing.[6]

The key point is that external *liabilities* become a form of liquidity that can be used to acquire assets at home. Local actors such as the government may or may not be able to issue liabilities abroad denominated in domestic currency (such as government borrowing, $B^*$, in table 6.1). If they cannot, the limitation is quaintly called "original sin" in the academic literature. But Stage III sinners in good standing with their creditors are welcome to borrow in foreign currency terms. Unfortunately, this situation may not persist.

The presence of foreign liabilities in portfolios immediately exposes their holders to exchange rate risk due to currency misalignment—or mismatch. If their assets and expected net revenues are denominated in domestic currency, but their liabilities are denominated in foreign currency, then an increase in the exchange rate, $e$, generates both capital and income losses. The higher rate cuts directly into net worth and jacks up the cost of debt service. The threat to balance sheets is greater if (as has often been the case) there is a maturity mismatch involving short-term foreign liabilities and long-term domestic assets.

These dangers are especially grave for actors, such as firms producing nontraded goods and the government itself, insofar as their main sources of income are set in local currency. Although some assets of exporters (e.g., the real estate that they own and their deposits in the domestic financial system) may be denominated in local currency and be subject to the same problems, they could be more than offset by the larger domestic value of their current and expected net income in foreign currency.

Money and credit expansion attributable to the accumulation of international reserves during phases of booming capital inflows has become a persistent problem in emerging market economies.[7] If there is a market in domestic bonds, the central bank can in principle sterilize the monetary effect of international reserve accumulation by selling its own or government paper in exchange for money in an open market operation, although at the risk of driving up interest rates that may then bring in still more foreign capital.

Two other options for sterilization exist: reducing the public sector debt by running a budget surplus or accumulating the domestic money generated by the additional international reserves as deposit reserves of commercial banks. These options are the only ones available if there is no well-developed domestic debt market (that is, we are closer to Stage I in terms of domestic financing). A long sequence of currency crises shows that such interventions may be of limited effectiveness.

## Stage IV Finance

Use of liabilities as a source of liquidity expands greatly in Stage IV. A local market for equity issued by the private sector can provide the trampoline. This stage is where the most successful developing countries as well as some of the slow-growing regions (Central and Eastern Europe and the semi-industrialized countries, in particular) are placed now or toward which they are moving. Historically, the emergence of significant stock markets dates from the 1990s in many developing countries (with privatization of state enterprises often providing the impetus) and is fairly recent even in non–Anglo Saxon industrialized economies.

In table 6.1, the value of private sector shares outstanding is $P_V V$, with $P_V$ as a price index and $V$ a measure of outstanding volume.[8] In a wonderful seventeenth-century Dutch word, a Stage IV economy can enter into *windhandel*, or "wind trade," based on the use of liabilities (and derivatives built around them) as sources of liquidity. This possibility is reflected in table 6.1's "finance" sector, which holds shares, $P_V V_F$, financed by borrowing from banks and abroad (ignore the $QS_F$ term for the moment). The sector's equity or net worth is $\Omega_F$, held by the private sector as an asset.

Within the financial sector, there are offsetting asset and liability entries, $Z$. Individual financial actors such as broker-dealers, financial agents active in mortgage bond markets (e.g., some pension funds in developing countries or Fannie Mae and Freddie Mac in the United States), and hedge funds can borrow from one another, but for their subsystem as a whole many of these transactions will be mutually offsetting.[9] By increasing transactions such as $Z$, financial institutions can add to cash flow as they build up asset/equity or leverage ratios, $\lambda_F = (P_V V_F + Z)/\Omega_F$. The liabilities, $L_F + Z + eL_F^*$, underlying total assets, $P_V V_F + Z$, can support imposing structures of leverage and liquidity.[10]

So long as $P_V$ continues to rise, growing intrafinancial sector claims make it possible to mobilize large sums of money to buy stock. Of course, $P_V$ can also fall, precipitating a collapse. Again, appetite for risk during a boom becomes flight to quality in a crash marked by "deleveraging" or a contraction of liquidity in the form of liabilities and a retreat to assets such as government bonds and even money.

The financial sector can also be dependent on the rest of the world. If local operators borrow heavily from abroad ($eL_F^*$ in table 6.1) and invest at home, ample possibilities arise for currency and maturity misalignments in national balance sheets of the sort that led to the succession of emerging market financial crises in the 1990s.

Diversified finance as in Stage IV also creates opportunities. Somewhat surprisingly, firms in chapter 3's rapidly growing economies have relied on selling new shares for a significant portion of their investment finance, certainly not the practice in many advanced economies where share buybacks predominate (Singh 1995; Staritz 2008). Active stock markets also allow entrepreneurs to cash in on their innovations via initial public offerings (IPOs) of shares, a significant incentive for technological advance.

## Stage V Finance

Stage V finance—not yet significant in most developing economies—adds the contemporary twist of asset securitization. In just one of many possible examples, suppose that besides productive capital the private sector holds a tangible asset, $C$, with price, $P_C$ (the obvious example is residential housing). It borrows $M_P$ (for "mortgages") from banks, using $P_C C$ as collateral. The banks in turn bundle the mortgages into a security, $S$, with price, $Q$, which is sold to financial actors. Such maneuvers make it possible to borrow large sums of money and pump up leverage by increasing claims on the nonfinancial sector.

However, there are also problems with this. First, how to evaluate collateral for securitized loans is one problem. Aside from ample opportunities for fraud, a key point in recent U.S. experience is that the housing collateral for "subprime" mortgages was itself subject to capital gains and losses, and that the ability of the borrowers to be able to meet their payment obligations was open to question (without, needless to say, any prior provision being made on the part of the lenders during the upswing for the loan losses they were likely to incur during the succeeding downswing).[11] To the extent that these assets were traded, they were valued at market prices (mark-to-market). Rating agencies were asked to judge their quality before they were marketed and changed the rating through time. A capital gain on the primary asset (housing) led directly to a jump in the asset price, Q, which stimulated balance sheet expansion.

A second problem is that a large portion of these complex securities were not marketed. They were given a hypothetical valuation, Q, based on mathematical models internal to the financial institutions. These procedures were flawed, as we will see later in the chapter. But they were a wonderful source of liquidity until the bottom fell out of the subprime market, carrying down with it the values of securitized assets. Then a crisis hit, with drastic deleveraging and shrinkage of liquidity.

As this book went to the press, the industrialized economies are still sorting out the consequences of deleveraging Stage V. But it seems clear that public regulation of both bank and nonbank financial operations can help reduce the likelihood of booms and crashes. Financial safety nets can be constructed. However, when liquidity takes the form of liabilities that can be used to pay for profit seeking in financial markets (not to mention fees for the people who "guide" investors), sources of potential volatility will always appear, even in constricted early stage financial systems.

## Pro-Cyclical Regulatory Complications

Stage V but also Stages III and IV finance raises numerous problems of regulation. As previously noted, the Basel I and II standards concentrate on commercial bank capital. Besides issuing equity per se, banks also make provisions (or reserves) for expected losses in their loan portfolio. They are held in liquid assets and add to the net worth of the banks as they are built up, but are expected to be spent sometime in the future when losses are made. For simplicity in notation, we assume that they are part of bank capital, $\Omega_{comm}$. When a bank gets into trouble, it has to use the provisions it has accumulated or reduce its leverage by disposing of assets or building up equity. Cutting shareholder dividends and selling new stock are the usual mechanisms for the latter. Examples were rife in the industrialized economies in 2007–2008. For developing countries at higher stages of finance, the Basel methodology which sets targets for how much capital and provisions financial firms have to hold as backing for assets is increasingly relevant. We provide a brief sketch with emphasis on the problems it may present.[12]

Basel II rests on three "pillars," with the first being that a bank should maintain capital and provisions adequate to guarantee that if there is an adverse shock to its assets, there will be only a small probability of a loss. The bank's assets should be valued on the basis of market parameters (interest rates, expected losses given market conditions, etc.), including to the extent possible asset prices set in relevant markets that can be used to value such holdings (mark-to-market pricing).

Pillar One emphasizes that such calculations should be based on the bank's internal risk weighting models and could take into account the information provided by the ratings agencies. In developing countries, however, few assets are rated by these agencies. Some asset-backed securities are rated in industrial countries, but the more complex rarely trade, so there is no market on the basis of which to estimate values. Furthermore, even in industrial countries, the loan portfolio is not rated and is only imperfectly tradable. When it has to be sold during a crisis, discounts can be considerable.

The complicated mathematics used for asset valuation creates problems of its own. A major consideration is that going into the 2007 crisis, all financial institutions were using models based on the same theory (the basics involving comparisons of returns and risks described by hypothetically *known* probability distributions go back to Markowitz [1952]) and estimated using the same historical data. There was already a lot of homogeneity built into their market perceptions. Worse still, the models presuppose that financial actors can always trade at stable "market-determined" prices. As we previously pointed out, this assumption is inapplicable for many assets and, equally important, fails for those assets for which there is a market if all the players are thinking more or less the same thing and then change their minds in the same direction—not everybody can attempt to buy or sell at the same time without causing prices to move. Similar perceptions then lead to greater asset price volatility. Marking-to-market turns highly pro-cyclical, as assets are overpriced during booms but possibly underpriced in the environment of pessimism that prevails during crises.

Such herd behavior was exacerbated by Basel Pillar Three calling for market discipline enforced by greater disclosure of banks' financial status and their internal risk management procedures. Such measures were not the most effective means to confront *systemic* risk caused by the herding behavior previously discussed—an externality not encompassed by internal procedures and not accounted for in the market place. Pillar Two, supervision, could potentially deal with this problem, but evidence indicates that it is ignored or seriously underutilized until crises actually strike.

To understand in a more formal way the source of the problem, we should observe that major financial actors generally operated on the basis of "value at risk," or $V$ as estimated by their models. Value at risk is linked to the equity capital, $\Omega$, that the firm must hold to stay solvent with high probability (Adrian and Shin 2008). Firms presumably adjust their balance sheets to target a ratio of economic capital, $\Omega$ to $V$, say:

$$\Omega = \theta V.$$

With $A$ as their assets, leverage $\lambda$ then becomes

$$\lambda = \frac{A}{\Omega} = \left(\frac{1}{\theta}\right)\left(\frac{A}{V}\right). \tag{1}$$

These are all *static* relationships, supported by models with probability distributions estimated from existing data at a point in time. The dangers they create result from their impacts on the *dynamic* behavior of financial firms. The heart of the matter is that leverage responds *inversely* to asset price increases. In highly simplified form, a firm's balance sheet can be written as

$$A = D + \Omega$$

with $D$ as debt.

Suppose that there is a capital gain on a firm's assets. If debt stays constant for the moment, equity, $\Omega$, will rise by an equal *absolute* amount. Because $\Omega \ll A$ for financial firms, the *proportional* increase in $\Omega$ markedly exceeds that in $A$. Hence leverage, or $\lambda = A/\Omega$, goes down. Financial firms then have a strong incentive to increase debt to buy additional assets to build up leverage, engaging in windhandel to profit from increased cash flow while still respecting preset limits on risk. In the subprime mortgage adventure, firms were typically borrowing short-term to acquire long-term assets in anticipation of capital gains—back to the Mississippi and South Sea Companies of 300 years ago!

So what happens if asset prices go down? Leverage jumps up, and from equation (1), $\frac{V}{A}$ increases for a given $\theta$. With greater value at risk relative to assets, Basel rules obligate the firm to reduce leverage by disposing of assets or building up equity. If firms are largely similar and react in much the same way to an adverse shock, the resulting fire sale of assets can lead to dramatic price reductions and a liquidity conflagration as in 2007–2008.

As we will see in chapter 7, there are ways to attenuate this behavior, basically building rules that try to correct for the pro-cyclical behavior of financial and asset markets. In practice, in industrial and developing countries alike, crises hit when financial institutions are seriously undercapitalized (after all, undercapitalization is the other side of the coin of large profits made during the boom on the basis of high leverage). The sales of assets in markets with one-sided expectations then lead to losses that further feed into expectations and market valuations. The final result is a credit crunch.

## Notes

1. A natural extension would be to split the private sector into households and business. However, to simplify the exposition, further breakdown of the private sector is not pursued in this chapter. IMF financial programming and monetarist macroeconomics often consolidate the commercial and central banks into one sector. However, to allow us to bring in relevant monetary policy issues, we keep them separated in table 6.1.
2. As is often the case in macroeconomic modeling for the moment, we ignore bank equity, $\Omega_{comm}$, held by the private sector as an asset. It is brought into the discussion about financial regulation later in the chapter.
3. Standard definitions of "high-powered money" also include currency and coins, which we omit to save on symbols. They were key components of the rich countries' financial systems well into the nineteenth century and remain important in many developing economies today.
4. Kindleberger and Aliber (2005) is the classic narrative.
5. The "assets" might be claims on hypothetical future revenue streams (the South Sea and Mississippi cases discussed below) or equity of former state enterprises (a standard case in late twentieth century developing country events).
6. The World Bank's database on *Financial Structure* (World Bank 2006) provides indicators on the size of equity and public and private bond markets for both developed and developing countries. These indicators can be used to group regions and countries according to the stages of finance described in the text.
7. If the exchange rate, $e$, stays constant, the home country's net foreign assets, $e(R^* - L^*) - B^* - P_V V^*$, can only change gradually over time via a surplus or deficit on current account. Hence a jump in foreign lending, $eL^*$ or $B^*$, must be met by an equal increase in reserves, $R^*$, which can stimulate money and credit expansion through the usual channels.
8. For the private nonfinancial sector, table 6.1 follows the accounting convention of the flow of funds by treating equity outstanding as a "liability" and allowing nonzero net worth. To illustrate a point made earlier, in flow-of-funds terms Google has highly negative net worth because its stock market valuation vastly exceeds its tangible capital and financial assets. On a balance sheet set up to follow accountants' conventions, Google like all other corporations would have zero net worth.
9. They may not offset completely. In available U.S. flow-of-funds data, for example, leveraged financial institutions typically have negative *net* positions in fed funds and security repurchase (repo) agreements. *Gross* repo asset and liability positions are not reported.
10. In the United States at the end of 2007, leverage for households was around 1.2, for commercial banks it was about 10, and for investment banks it was over 30.
11. In U.S. usage, subprime mortgages are not of sufficient quality to be bought and securitized by the government-sponsored enterprises Fannie Mae and Freddie Mac. Their securitization was undertaken by the private financial sector.
12. There is an enormous literature on the Basel standards. Our discussion draws heavily on Alexander et al. (2008).

# CHAPTER 7

# Macroeconomic Policy Choices

W HAT OPTIONS do the economic authorities in developing economies have for policy formation, at the macro and sectoral levels? Limits on policy maneuverability vary greatly across economies. In this chapter, we try to sort out the possibilities regarding macroeconomic regulation and then take up growth and sectoral policy in chapter 8.

We start by looking at how private and government net-borrowing flows and current account balances interact in the short-to-medium run. Some algebraic backup is provided in appendix 7.1, which deals with gap models, relationships between flow and stock variables, and theories of the exchange rate.

Macroeconomic policy packages appropriate to combinations of financial stages and binding gaps are reviewed. The discussion then turns to capital management techniques, including controlling international flows and regulating domestic financial markets, and central issues of financial development. The chapter closes with considerations regarding foreign aid.

## Pro-Cyclical Macroeconomic Adjustment and the Three Gaps

Patterns of net borrowing as presented in chapter 5 are a useful starting point for analyzing macroeconomic developments. As detailed in appendix 7.1, these flows cumulate into changes in balance sheets of the sort appearing in table 6.1, weaving a tight web between the real and financial sides of the economy.

If a sector has positive net borrowing, it is adding to effective demand because its expenditure exceeds its income. On the other hand, the sum of all sectors' net borrowings must be zero as a condition for macroeconomic equilibrium, i.e.

Net Private Borrowing + Government Borrowing + Current Account Balance = 0.

(The current account is, of course, also "foreign net borrowing"—that is, net borrowing by the rest of the world from the country whose accounts we are looking at.)

It is also helpful to consider how net borrowing flows might behave out of equilibrium. For example, would an increase in private income induce private spending to rise by more or less than the income increase itself? A greater increase in spending than income means that the private sector behaves "pro-cyclically"; a lesser increase is "counter-cyclical." A moment's thought suggests that if out-of-equilibrium *total* net borrowing behaves pro-cyclically, then the macro system is bound for trouble. A small income increase will kick up spending by a greater amount, which will presumably bid up output and income still more, and so on. This sort of instability is never observed, so it is safe to conclude that total net borrowing is in fact counter-cyclical.

Figure 7.1 illustrates a situation in which all three sectoral net-borrowing flows are counter-cyclical—i.e., when income goes up, private expenditure rises by a lesser amount (or investment increases by less than saving), exports grow

FIGURE 7.1

## Counter-cyclical net borrowing

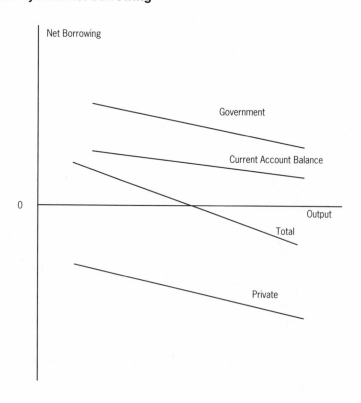

less than imports (so that the current account balance deteriorates), and taxes rise more than government spending. The curve for total net borrowing is just the vertical sum of the three sectoral curves. The point at which it crosses the horizontal axis is the equilibrium level of output.

The private sector in figure 7.1 has a surplus (negative net borrowing) and lends to the government and to the rest of the world. If the private net-borrowing curve shifts upward (the private surplus falls due to an investment increase, for example), then so would the total. The economy would arrive at a new equilibrium with a *higher* output level (a point to the right of the initial equilibrium) associated with a *lower* fiscal deficit and current account balance.

In practice, not all observed sectoral levels of net borrowing are counter-cyclical. For example, in data for the United States with the private sector separated into households and business, only the government behaves counter-cyclically, the two private subsectors are pro-cyclical, and the current account is basically a-cyclical (Barbosa-Filho et al., 2008). Several of the regions illustrated in chapter 5 face a similar phenomenon: private net borrowing tends to increase during upswings.

The macroeconomic implications are sketched in figure 7.2, in which the private sector behaves pro-cyclically with the other two counter-cyclically. The total net-borrowing curve still has a negative slope, but it is very shallow. An increase in private borrowing will again shift the total curve upward, leading to higher output. Because the slope of the total curve is so shallow, the output increase would be very large and could hit resource limits, kicking off inflation or an external crisis, due in the latter case to a sharp deterioration in the current account. In short, pro-cyclical spending by the private sector generates strong business cycle swings and creates additional risks of inflation and/or balance-of-payments crises.

The dire situation in figure 7.2 would be even more likely if the government itself behaves pro-cyclically, as discussed in chapter 1. Offsetting policies are possible but difficult, as discussed later in this chapter.

Stemming from the work of Hollis Chenery (e.g., Chenery and Bruno 1962), there is a long tradition in development economics devoted to the analysis of net-borrowing functions in the form of "gaps."[1] The terminology is meant to suggest that an excessively large positive level of net borrowing by the private sector (the "resource or savings gap") or the government (the "fiscal gap"), or a large current account deficit (the "external gap") is likely to lead the economy into trouble. Empirical gap analysis of net-borrowing flows as discussed in chapter 5 follows directly from Chenery's perspective.

For example, we can consider the circa 1980 interest rate shock discussed in chapter 2, accompanied by a virtual cutoff of new foreign lending. A country such as Brazil, which previously had a big current account deficit and was taking on more debt, even to finance its debt service obligations,[2] had to transfer

**FIGURE 7.2**

## Pro-cyclical near instability

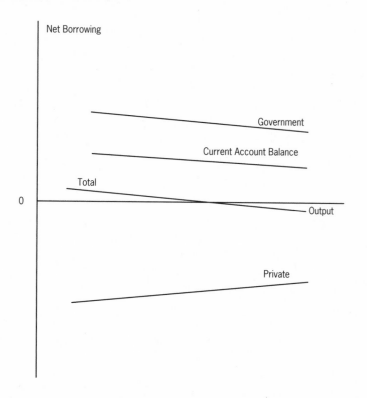

the hard currency service obligations abroad out of its own resources. More-over, in the aftermath of the shock, most countries effectively nationalized the debt that had been taken out by the private (or public enterprise) sector and shifted the burden to the government.

The repercussions were rather complicated, but a typical set can be traced in figure 7.3. Initial conditions include highly pro-cyclical private sector net borrowing and large external and fiscal gaps. The schedule for the current ac-count shifts upward because net new external borrowing becomes impossible (aside from "informal" loans in the form of increased payment arrears). Super-ficially, this looks like an improvement in external balance that should lead to an increase in effective demand, but appearances are deceiving in this case. Net exports are not going up; rather what is required is a greater transfer of re-sources abroad. Basically that transfer has to be accomplished by cutting im-ports to satisfy the (now) binding foreign exchange constraint, although real devaluation and directed policy can also reduce import demand for a given level of output and increase export supply.

**FIGURE 7.3**

## Reactions to an adverse external shock

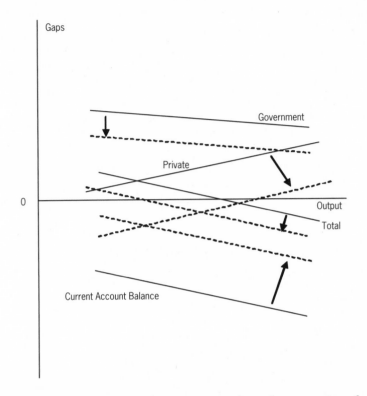

The most effective way to reduce imports is through contraction of aggregate demand. The question at hand is how the reduction will be allocated between the fiscal and the private resource gaps. A complicating factor is that imports of capital goods are likely to be an important component of total investment, so that reducing the resource gap by curtailing new capital formation may be an effective means to satisfy the external constraint. Of course, with investment slashed, future growth prospects will be hurt.

As figure 7.3 is drawn, government net borrowing declines modestly because it has assumed the private sector's debt service. The rest of the adjustment burden is carried by the private sector, which may take place through reductions in consumption imposed by the inflation tax. An inflation-induced cut in real wages (generating "forced savings") can also play a central role in reducing real private consumption. In the diagram as drawn, the private sector shifts from being a net borrower to a net lender. The fiscal gap declines but remains positive. Because the total net-borrowing schedule has a shallow negative slope, there is a substantial output reduction.

Run in reverse, figure 7.3 shows one possible response to a foreign exchange bonanza that allows a much bigger external deficit. The real question is, how long can favorable conditions be maintained?

In summary, two crucial stabilization problems that developing countries may confront are a binding external gap (which can arise either due to adverse developments such as plummeting terms of trade on the current account or—more common in recent years—destabilizing capital movements) and pro-cyclical behavior on the part of the private or public sector. There is also the possibility of pro-cyclical financial destabilization as discussed in chapter 6. What sorts of policies can be deployed to stabilize the macro system under combinations of these circumstances?

To answer the latter question, we look first at macroeconomic policy, and then at capital management (capital account and prudential regulations). A third form of intervention, focused on financial sector development, was analyzed in chapter 6.

## Macroeconomic Policies

### Counter-Cyclical Fiscal Policy

As we have seen, pro-cyclical private and government behavior can easily destabilize the economy. A first rule of macroeconomic policy is, therefore, that the government should avoid pro-cyclical fiscal policy and rather run it in the opposite fashion to counter pro-cyclical private sector behavior. As we will see in the following sections, in economies that have opened their capital account, counter-cyclical monetary policy faces severe constraints, and therefore, the need for a fiscal policy that tries to smooth the business cycle is even more acute. However, putting in place counter-cyclical fiscal policies is not an easy task.

One possibility is the use of fiscal stabilization funds to "store" temporary revenue upswings from taxes on raw material exports with surging prices. Well-designed tax systems, which capture in taxes a significant part of the upswings in incomes (for example, progressive income tax schemes) are an essential ingredient for such counter-cyclical management—obviously, if they are not spent. The funds could then be accumulated as foreign exchange reserves, or in sovereign wealth funds, which, as we will see in the following sections, also provide "self-insurance" against sudden stops in external financing as well as export price collapses. More aggressive counter-cyclical policies could take the form of taxes on exports and capital inflows (the unremunerated reserve requirements on capital inflows imposed by central banks, which we will discuss later, have an equivalent effect).

There is also the possibility of adjusting government outlays counter-cyclically, but long debates over "fine tuning" suggest that discretionary changes in public spending may be difficult to use effectively, as they involve significant lags in the approval and implementation process. *Automatic* stabilizers are much better. A well-designed safety net to protect vulnerable groups during crises (preferably as part of a permanent social protection system) is an automatic stabilizer that can play beneficial macroeconomic and social roles. This safety net is a major mechanism in industrial countries in the form of unemployment insurance.

Although they are difficult to design and apply in practice, setting up rules for balancing the government deficit over the cycle is also a desirable policy goal. The most appropriate rule in this regard is one establishing that the government would aim at a sustainable "structural" deficit—that is, a deficit adjusted to pro-cyclical swings in tax revenues and the costs of safety nets used as automatic stabilizers. If such a rule is followed, spending, excluding that associated with safety nets, would follow a long-term steady pace, and current fiscal deficits would fall during booms and increase during crisis. In the graphical representation of figures 7.1 to 7.3, the government net-borrowing requirements would have a steeper negative slope.

This rule could be mixed with another one, which would target a deficit equivalent to public sector investment requirements. This mixture would make the rule equivalent to what the British came to call the fiscal "golden rule"— essentially, the government only borrows in the long term to invest.

In any case, neither the golden nor the structural rule should avoid the use of fiscal policy as a strong stabilization devise when needed. Discretionary public sector spending policies would be called to support an economic recovery when private demand is very weak as well as to make cuts in spending to moderate aggregate demand when private spending is exuberant. Tax cuts and hikes can also play those roles through the cycles. However, changes in public sector spending have a direct effect on aggregate demand, whereas variations in taxes have only an indirect effect.

## *Interest Rates*

As argued in chapter 1, low and stable real interest rates can support investment in productive capacity and growth. However, a major challenge of monetary policy is that open capital markets in effect put a floor under local rates and generate pro-cyclical behavior.

The reasons rest upon straightforward financial arbitrage. Consider an investor comparing borrowing costs within the country and in foreign markets. In local currency terms, the real cost of funds for loans from abroad will be the base foreign borrowing rate (such as dollar LIBOR at a "normal" precrisis level of about 3 percent per year in mid-2008) *plus* the market risk premium for the country concerned (about 2 percent) *plus* the *expected* nominal rate of depreciation, which increases the local cost of paying off the loan in dollars.[3]

For a "typical" country, the sum of these three items prior to the 2007–2008 crisis might have been 8–10 percent, but in the not-so-distant past or after the September 2008 financial meltdown, it could easily have exceeded 20 percent, because both risk premia and expected depreciation were higher. This borrowing cost acts as a floor for interest rates in local currency, which we can refer to as the "parity" interest rate. Imperfect competition in the banking sector and high reserve requirements on deposits could work together to raise lending rates above the floor and drive deposit rates below it.

The major complication is that risk premia for developing countries tend to increase during crisis, at the same time that the scarcity of foreign exchange generates exchange rate depreciation. The result is that the floor for domestic interest rates tends to increase at the time when the economy enters into a recession, tending to worsen it. In turn, when external financing is abundant, risk premia tend to fall and exchange rate depreciation pressures moderate or are replaced by appreciation. So, parity interest rates tend to fall when the economy expands rapidly. If such a trend is transmitted domestically, it would further fuel the boom. These pro-cyclical swings in parity interest rates[4] are a major reason why the curve for the private sector gap tends to have the positive slope depicted in figures 7.2 and 7.3 rather than the negative slope of figure 7.1. The result, as we have seen, is that economic activity fluctuates more through the business cycle.

## Inflation Targeting

Pro-cyclical swings in interest rates are just the opposite of the standard counter-cyclical prescription for monetary management. It says that rates should be reduced during crises and increased during booms. In an economy with Stage II (or higher) finance, open market operations by the central bank are the instrument of choice.

Current orthodoxy has abandoned simple monetarist inflation models in favor of "inflation targeting." The theory first appeared in industrialized economies. It amounts to a *bossa nova* riff on Say's Law.[5] Full employment of labor is now called a NAIRU (non-accelerating inflation rate of unemployment), an acronym only an economist could love. Estimating the NAIRU econometrically turns out to be difficult, if only because it is an intercept term in a regression equation for the inflation rate. The first thing one learns in elementary econometrics is that intercept terms jump around a lot.

Be that as it may, under the now widely accepted "Taylor rule," the central bank is supposed to reduce the short-term interest rate when inflation falls below an unstated or pre-announced target and, in the opposite case, to increase the rate when inflation is above the target.[6] If inflation is determined exclusively by demand, this turns out to be a counter-cyclical rule. In a simplistic model, inflation would rise when unemployment falls below its NAIRU level and increase when it is above it. The rule would therefore tend to stabilize un-employment around the NAIRU level. An "independent" central bank (basi-cally meaning that the bank does not report directly to the Ministry of Fi-nance) is supposed to lend credibility to the inflation target.

The counter-cyclical effect may be absent if the source of rising inflation is not domestic demand but a supply shock, such as the sharp oil and food price hikes of the first half of 2008. A simple rule would be that the central bank should simply ignore these shocks as temporary. But if it fears that they will generate additional increases in wages and prices (the so called "second-round effects"), which risk transforming the price shock into permanent acceleration in inflation, it would try to counteract the price hikes by increasing the interest rate. The result is that the central bank would transform the supply shock into a reduction of economic activity.

In developing countries, not much attention is paid to the NAIRU, and any monetary analysis must bring the exchange rate and capital flows into the pic-ture. These generate two major complications. First of all and as previously noted, *counter*-cyclical interest rate policy goes against the logic of *pro*-cyclical swings in parity interest rates. By trying to increase domestic interest rates during booms, when parity rates tend to fall, the central bank would generate a great inducement to additional capital inflows, which would in turn rein-force the tendency of the exchange rate to appreciate. The opposite is true dur-ing crises, when reductions in domestic interest rates could encourage capital flight, as parity rates increase.

The second complication is that the exchange rate enters into the forma-tion of domestic prices, directly through imported and exported consumer goods, and indirectly through the cost structure of firms that import inputs for their production. This linkage belongs to the category of supply shocks on the price level previously discussed, which are favorable during booms. The stron-ger currency leads to slower inflation and helps the central bank meet its target. Joint appreciation and capital inflows can lead to a boom with low inflation, but only at the cost of growing external deficits that create vulnerability to a sudden stop in external financing.

The other way around, during downswings, attempts to reduce the interest rate would tend to reinforce depreciation pressures and induce additional capi-tal outflows. The effects of exchange rate depreciation on domestic prices now operate as an adverse supply shock and may lead monetary authorities follow-ing inflation targeting to increase rather than reduce interest rates, thus rein-forcing the recession.

Therefore, so long as the logic of parity interest rates is pro-cyclical, the capac-ity of central banks to manage rates in a counter-cyclical fashion is limited and may actually reinforce the pro-cyclicality of capital flows—and, therefore, of private sector net borrowing and associated spending—and generate exchange rate volatility. Because of the effects of the exchange rate on the domestic price level, the monetary authorities may in practice (as in Brazil and Mexico, for example[7]) fight depreciation during crisis but tolerate appreciation during booms. This would tend to generate high average interest rates and a strong exchange rate over the business cycle, to the detriment of real economic activity.

In sum, pro-cyclical swings in parity interest rates reduce the room to maneuver of monetary authorities to undertake truly counter-cyclical policy. The other side of the same coin is that authorities may simply shift the problem to the exchange rate. In the current account, appreciation during booms tends to generate large deficits that make the economy extremely vulnerable to sharp reversals in the availability and/or cost of external financing. As previously noted, a positive slope of the private sector net-borrowing schedule may be the result, which results in turn in large swings in economic activity.

The only way to break the deadlock involves a mix of two complementary policies. The first is to smooth out exchange rate swings, through heavy intervention in foreign exchange markets. The second is to delink, at least partially, the association between domestic and parity interest rates through capital account regulations. We now turn our attention to these issues.

## Foreign Exchange Reserve Management

From a stabilization perspective, the basic rationale for heavy intervention in foreign exchange markets comes clearly from the previous discussion: it helps smooth out the effects of strong external shocks generated by swings in external financing (that is, persistent shocks on the current account curve in figures 7.1 to 7.3), and helps in particular to avoid the strong swings in parity interest rates, as the exchange rate is one of its determinants. In addition, there are additional justifications for such interventions from a developmental perspective.

Reserve accumulation during booms should therefore help smooth out the effects of pro-cyclical capital flows on exchange rates. If adequately sterilized, such policy would make it possible to target *both* the exchange rate and the interest rate, thus avoiding the "trilemma" of open economies.[8] A similar logic applies to primary commodity exporting countries facing terms-of-trade shocks. Indeed, saving some of the exceptional export revenues and associated fiscal revenues is a good practice, as previously noted. More generally, it can be argued that cyclical swings in export revenues should be managed through cyclical swings in foreign exchange reserves (or sovereign wealth funds) that would accumulate the excess supply of foreign exchange during booms to be used during the succeeding crises.

The very strong crises of the late 1990s led developing countries to use this policy instrument in an active and in some cases aggressive way. The Asian countries led the way, but the trend was much broader and massive.[9] The use of this policy instrument was also a response to the Asian and Russian crises of

1997 and 1998, which revealed the lack of adequate institutions to manage crises that originated in sudden stops in external financing, as well as the excessive conditionalities associated with those that were available, mostly emergency IMF financing. In other words, in the absence of collective insurance provided by an international institution (the type of insurance that governments and central banks provide to financial systems domestically), "self-insurance" became the only available option to manage sharp swings in external financing.

Self-insurance against financial crises requires that countries should keep foreign exchange reserves at least equivalent to short-term external liabilities, which can easily fly away during crises (this is called the Guidotti-Greenspan rule). But it should certainly go beyond it, because long-term capital flows can also be sharply cut during crises. The precautionary demand for international reserves should therefore be proportional to *total* external liabilities, a proportion which furthermore should be larger the more open the capital account is.[10]

Exchange rate intervention also has developmental objectives that go beyond smoothing the effects of capital account fluctuations (and, no doubt, include some "mercantilist" motives). As we will see in chapters 8 and 9, a competitive exchange rate may have positive effects on growth. Avoiding sharp fluctuations in real exchange rates is also crucial to give stable incentives to exporters and producers of goods and services that compete with imports— that is to producers of tradable goods and services. These two motivations are, of course, interrelated, as reduced price volatility for tradables encourages investment in those sectors. Avoiding, in particular, natural resource and capital account booms from generating a strong appreciation of the exchange rate that destroys nonnatural resource sector production and export sectors (the Dutch disease again) is crucial.

The drawback of interventions in foreign exchange markets is, of course, that reserve accumulation is expensive because the riskless hard currency securities in which developing countries invest their reserves pay very low real interest rates and are subject to the volatility of exchange rates among major currencies. Furthermore, reserve increases must often be sterilized to avoid sharp swings in domestic money supply and lending (see chapter 6). If central bank or government bonds are used as the sterilization instrument, the associated interest rates are commonly higher than the returns from investing the reserves abroad, and thus generate losses for central banks (usually called "quasi-fiscal" deficits).

## Capital Management Techniques

Liquidity transformations, as discussed in chapter 6, have been a prime source of instability in developing economies. Together with liquid assets such as international reserves, countries' liability structures play a crucial role when there are external constraints. Particularly, if there is a sudden stop in external financing, short-term capital is likely to fly away rapidly. They also affect the behavior of private sector net-borrowing requirements, tending to make them pro-cyclical. Foreign exchange reserves can serve as a protection mechanism to manage these swings, but it is an expensive one, as previously indicated. Capital account regulation then becomes an essential policy tool to manage these destabilizing effects.

## Capital Account Regulations

Viewed as a debt management instrument, capital controls build on the fact that the market penalizes unsound external debt profiles. During booms, regulations should therefore be aimed at improving the debt maturity profiles of external liabilities of both the public and private sectors. As a liability (not figuring explicitly in table 6.1), foreign direct investment has also proven to be less volatile than portfolio and debt flows and creates risk sharing between domestic and foreign investors. On the other hand, FDI generally carries higher costs than other forms of external financing.

Viewed as a macroeconomic policy instrument, capital account regulation aims at reducing unstable international financial flows, often the root cause of boom-bust cycles, and at increasing the room to maneuver for monetary authorities. It can help them "lean against the wind" in an upswing by permitting contractionary monetary policy and reducing pressure for appreciation. Costly reserve accumulation and sterilization can also be held down. In a crisis, capital controls can create room for expansionary monetary policy. In either direction, regulation can help the authorities combine counter-cyclical monetary policy with active exchange rate targeting for developmental purposes.

In practice, capital market regulations *segment* domestic and international markets, but this reflects the fact that markets are themselves segmented. The strong pro-cyclical flows toward developing countries are indeed a consequence of segmentation, in which developing countries are perceived as "risky" borrowers and thus receive large flows during periods in which financial market agents have "appetite for risk" but are then subject to sudden stops when there is "flight to quality" (see chapter 1).

Traditional "quantity" controls of the type used in China and India (but being gradually dismantled in these countries, as in others before) openly differentiate between residents and nonresidents, and between corporate and noncorporate agents among the former. Prohibitions or ceilings may be imposed on foreign borrowing by domestic residents, or on foreign investors taking positions in domestic securities. There may be limitations on various forms of lending and borrowing in foreign currency by banks.

"Market-based" controls, practiced in recent decades in Latin America and Malaysia, include taxes or an unremunerated reserve requirement (URR) on inflows, and exit taxes on outflows. Market-based instruments tend to be more nondiscretionary than direct methods.

Following Ocampo (2008), a large literature on these experiences leads to five main conclusions:

1. Controls on both inflows and outflows can work, but the authorities must be able to administer regulation while closing loopholes and (especially) avoiding corruption. *Permanent* regulatory regimes that can be tightened or loosened in response to market conditions, including the cycle, are probably preferable to repeated retractions and reinstatements of the rules.

2. Exchange controls and quantitative restrictions may be the best means to hold down domestic sensitivity to international capital flows (witness China's and India's avoidance of the Asian crisis in the late 1990s[11]). In contrast, URRs and similar measures may have only temporary effects on capital inflows (especially if they are not ratcheted up during a surge), but they do influence interest rate spreads and, in this sense, are a useful complement to counter-cyclical macroeconomic policies.

3. URRs and other reserve requirements help hold down short-term debt, which is highly volatile and thus a significant source of vulnerability.

4. To guarantee that capital market regulations can be effective, some intervention in current account transactions may be required as well. Export surrender obligations or requirements to channel trade transactions through approved intermediaries are examples in point.

5. Perhaps most important, controls are a complement to other macro policies, for both stabilization and maintenance of sound macro prices, not a substitute for them.

Capital controls obviously have costs. They increase the cost of financing during surges, but that is precisely what they are supposed to do. In the longer term, they can inhibit the development of derivatives markets and discourage operations by foreign institutional investors who may act as domestic market makers. The trade-offs between short-term effectiveness of capital controls and their possibly unfavorable long-term repercussions are not simple but do have to be borne in mind.

## Prudential Regulation

The distinction between capital account and prudential regulations affecting cross-border flows is not clear-cut. Both instruments are aimed at making the financial system more stable and effective.

One area of concern is foreign currency borrowing by nonfinancial firms that have no revenues in foreign currency—that is, that produce nontradable goods and services.[12] Various restrictions can be imagined, but perhaps the simplest is prohibiting firms without foreign currency revenues from borrowing abroad or domestically in foreign currency. Alternatively, price-based penalties on such borrowing can be imposed.

The macroeconomic risks we have analyzed should also be a central concern of prudential regulation, as they affect the health of the financial system. Traditionally, microeconomic risk management has been directed toward reducing the risks that depend on the characteristics of individual borrowers. But additional sources of risk are associated with economic policy changes (e.g., changes in interest and exchange rates), volatility in external financing, and pro-cyclical private sector behavior, particularly during boom periods.

The situation is made worse by the pro-cyclicality of traditional regulatory tools, including the international standards issued by the Basel Committee on Banking Supervision. To add to the discussion of pro-cyclical leverage in chapter 6, it is helpful to work through an example involving loan-loss provisions (or reserves), which tend to be tied to current delinquencies or short-term expectations about them. In an upswing delinquencies are low; this fact and the consequent need to make limited provisions can encourage risk taking. In a crisis, a jump in delinquencies rapidly exhausts existing provisions. Financial institutions will have to use their capital to cover losses, but then, given regulatory capital requirements, their capacity to lend is limited and may therefore trigger a credit squeeze. They could also sell some of their assets, but this is hardly a solution when many financial institutions want to do it at the same time. The fire sale of the assets under these conditions generates considerable losses and thus a credit squeeze is not spared. Needless to say, such problems can be especially severe in developing countries just entering into Stage IV and V finance.

Most banks and other financial institutions tend to make provisions close in time to when loans are supposed to come due and are not expected to be paid. The insurance industry, however, makes provisions when an insurance policy is issued. The analog for banks would be to build up provisions when loans are *disbursed* rather than when repayments (or, rather the lack of repayments) are expected. This sort of action counters the financial cycle, because it amounts to an increase in the banks' own funds ($\Omega_{comm}$ in table 6.1) during boom, which will give them more room for maneuver to manage losses during crises.

Under this system, provisions build up during an upswing and can be accumulated in a fund (along with special backup for nonperforming assets or borrowers under stress). The fund can be drawn down in a slump to cover loan and other asset losses. This system would be only cycle-neutral, as it essentially follows the pro-cyclicality of lending, but still would be a considerable advance over current practices. This practice was introduced by Spain in 2000. An alternative, which some analysts have suggested recently, is to increase capital requirements during booms, that is, to force financial institutions to increase $\Omega_{comm}$ through explicit capital injections and not through provisions.[13]

More direct counter-cyclical rules regarding changes in the credit exposure of financial institutions would also be desirable. In particular, general or sector-specific increases in provisions could be forced onto financial agents when there is an excessive growth of credit relative to a benchmark, a bias in lending toward sectors subject to strong cyclical swings, and (again) growth in foreign currency loans to sectors producing nontradable goods and services. Indeed, all currency mismatches on balance sheets as well as in expected income and payment flows are hazardous and should be subject to provisions.[14]

A final and crucial issue for counter-cyclical management is mark-to-market pricing of assets. This practice is good from the point of view of transparency of the balance sheets of financial agents, but has strong pro-cyclical effects, as asset prices (for stocks and real estate) are strongly pro-cyclical. A similar effect is associated with the prices of assets that serve as loan collateral. If no relevant market happens to be at hand (as was the case for complex instruments such as collateralized debt obligations), regulations usually require that prices be constructed using models, with the consequences described in chapter 6. During booms, both practices feed into a credit boom based on capital gains that have a high cyclical component. During crises, the associated capital losses force financial institutions to sell some assets, but the fire sale of such assets worsens the problem, as previously indicated.

Thus, even if mark-to-market continues to be preferred for transparency reasons, some mechanism has to be introduced to avoid cyclical price booms from feeding into leverage, such as limits on the values of assets that can be used as a backing for credit or bond issues. For institutions in trouble during crises, "regulatory forbearance" in the sense of not imposing mark-to-market in a downswing might be appropriate, though it also has its downsides.[15] In any case, regulations which act counter-cyclically in a downswing (such as regulatory forbearance) and do nothing in an upswing do not encourage prudential private sector behavior. Hence, the regulatory design has to be symmetrical.

## Foreign Aid

To close this discussion and lay the ground for the analysis in chapter 6, it makes sense to take a look at foreign aid. Aid largely flows to economies with Stage I (or at most, Stage II) financial structures. In table 6.1, it allows the government to take on more foreign loans, $eL_G^*$, and reduce its borrowing, $B_{comm}$ and $B_{cent}$, from the banks, presumably with stabilizing monetary consequences.

Its immediate macroeconomic impacts are visualized in figures 7.1 and 7.2. The extra resources allow the government net-borrowing schedule to shift upward via greater spending or tax cuts. The latter would also stimulate private net borrowing directly. The two upward shifts would lead to higher imports and the current account curve would shift down to hold the total equal to zero. The new schedule for total borrowing would shift upward, leading to a higher level of output to the right of the initial equilibrium.

In effect, the economy is reconfigured to absorb a continuing financial inflow. Risks such as an outburst of Dutch disease generated by the exchange rate appreciation induced by the additional foreign exchange are, of course, a potential outcome. Even if they can be avoided, what would be the implications of increased donor contributions for per capita economic growth? We have already gone over much of the ground, but it makes sense to revisit it from the angle of aid, which has many contradictory aspects.

A well-known adage from Lao Tzu provides a concise description of two implications: "Give a man a fish and you feed him for a day" means that external assistance can be a dole. But its true purpose is presumably to "teach a man (or a national economy) to fish and . . . feed him for a lifetime." As pointed out in chapter 1, a rule of thumb for successful "fishing" is that the economy sustain at least 2 percent annual per capita output growth. Employment creation should keep pace with rising population.

Beyond Lao Tzu's distinction, foreign aid has other complications. It certainly has helped launch 2 percent or faster per capita growth performances in diverse policy environments. As has been stressed repeatedly, limited availability of hard currency is often the crucial bottleneck in a developing economy, holding down both supply and demand. If, as in the previous discussion, effective demand can increase because foreign exchange is available to pay for the associated imports, it can stimulate private sector investment and innovation. At the same time, the imports can bring in essential goods and technologies to raise productive capacity. The following are examples:

The first, most successful aid efforts were the post–World War II Marshall Plan in Europe and the parallel reconstruction program in Japan. They emphasized breaking foreign exchange bottlenecks (the "dollar shortage") via coordinated public and private interventions as opposed to the more recent obsession with market liberalization. It is worth recalling that the Americans who helped implement reconstruction were New Dealers at ease with an interventionist state.

In the 1960s and 1970s illiberal and bureaucratically planned South Korea utilized capital inflows and American-guaranteed market access to create a formidable industrial base, beginning with textiles and going on to the world's biggest integrated steel plant and beyond into chip manufacture, automobiles, and broadband Internet coverage for over 90 percent of the country. Korea's international economic situation was a consequence of cold war politics, but its planners took full advantage of the opportunities they had available.

In the "lost decade" of the 1980s, Chile performed better than the rest of Latin America because it received ample foreign assistance from international financial institutions favoring its neoliberal policy stance. Increasingly sophisticated natural resource–based exports supported economic expansion.

Several economies in sub-Saharan Africa now have respectable growth rates with support from Nordic and other donors who provided steady aid flows over decades for their own geopolitical reasons.

In all these countries, big shifts in economic structure were created by a combination of technocratic top-down policy and spontaneous innovation from the bottom up. Even in neoliberal Chile, the government consistently supported expansion of mineral and agro-exports. Nowadays, of course, mainstream opinion opposes state intervention, a viewpoint virtually ignored at the time of the Marshall Plan or South Korea's growth spurt.

Over the past two or three decades, many aid packages and economic "reform" programs informed by the Washington consensus did not generate linkages among demand growth, productivity, and employment. Per capita income levels did not rise and workers displaced by trade liberalization vanished into informal and subsistence activities. Under these conditions, foreign aid become at best a dole and at worst a cesspool for corruption.

Certainly, aid can have positive impacts at the micro level. A handout from abroad may cure smallpox or alleviate childhood malnutrition, but it is a handout notwithstanding. As chapter 3 shows, in recent decades many poor economies have seen marked improvements in primary education (and health care as well) but have not been able to grow. Even if commendable and successful on their own terms, people-oriented technical fixes at the household level (as advocated by Sachs 2005) may not directly stimulate economy-wide expansion and enduring poverty alleviation.

Looking toward the future, foreign assistance is bound to be available in limited quantities. Cost estimates for the Millennium Development Goals, which emphasize quick results, range upward from $150 billion per year. Current aid flows in principle now are on the order of $100 billion including debt relief and technical cooperation, which do not transfer resources to the recipient country. The International Monetary Fund has not been allowing governments to channel forgiven debt toward increased spending on poverty reduction because of its phobic fear (not supported by evidence) that an increase in fiscal outlays will kick off uncontrollable inflation.

Even if aid mounts, the IMF relents, and humanitarian goals are realized, the MDG effort can only be successful if it puts economies on paths of sustained growth. In the past, aid has sometimes set off growth, more often it hasn't. There are many challenges to overcome:

At the micro level, just by itself human capital augmentation will not support steady growth unless high productivity enterprises get started.

Entrepreneurship is essential to this end and should be rewarded.

But that will not happen spontaneously in a liberalized market environment. The state has to play a strong supportive role. Its available policy space has to expand so that countries can use instruments like sensible protection levels, targeted credit, and production subsidies to direct their limited resources toward productive ends. Scale economies are potentially available in many lines of endeavor—the task is to identify and support them. Linking fetters on developmentalist policies to disbursements of aid—standard practice for the World Bank and IMF—is completely counterproductive.

In recent years, many sub-Saharan African countries found a new solution: Chinese aid. Based on its own record of strong growth, this donor has of course no objections to a developmentalist state. It focuses on getting the economies to grow, based on exploiting the opportunities for raw material exports that China itself has generated. And it is not tied to the conditionality of the Bretton Woods Institutions.

## APPENDIX 7.1: NET BORROWING, BALANCE SHEETS, AND OPEN ECONOMY MACRO

The first topic in this appendix is how private, government, and the current account balance interact. We then show how borrowing flows cumulate into asset stocks as illustrated in table 6.1. Next we discuss the well-known Mundell-Fleming (or IS/LM/BP) and portfolio balance models from open economy macroeconomics, and how they underlie the (misleading) "trilemma" mentioned in chapter 1. The appendix closes with a discussion of dynamic, expectational forces that can affect the exchange rate. We work with annual flows of output, net borrowing, and other variables from the national income and product accounts along with relevant stocks from balance sheets. The symbols can be interpreted as being in current market prices or else as "real" (market price estimates deflated by a price index), as the situation warrants.

Recall from chapter 1 that in the national accounts national income is identified with national output. For present purposes, it makes sense to extend the accounting slightly to make total "supply," $X$, equal to value added, $Y$ (or GDP), generated within the economy, plus imports, $eM^*$, valued in home currency terms at the exchange rate, $e$ ($M^*$ stands for imports "at world prices"),

$$X = Y + eM^*. \tag{1}$$

The uses of supply are described by the equation

$$C+I+G+E-X=0, \tag{2}$$

with $C$ as private consumption, $I$ as investment (gross fixed capital formation plus inventory accumulation), $G$ as government spending on goods and services, and $E$ as exports.

The private sector's income-expenditure statement can be written as

$$N_p=I+C+T+Z_p-Y, \tag{3}$$

which says that the sector's net borrowing, $N_p$, is equal to its expenditure minus income. If outlays exceed inflows, the sector has to increase its net liabilities to the rest of the economy.[16]

The new entries are taxes, $T$, and a "transfer," $Z_p$, to the rest of the world, in terms of domestic prices. Examples are profit remittances and interest payments on foreign debt. If a transfer such as emigrant remittances is coming in, it adds to income and should be written as $-eZ_p^*$, with $Z_p^*$ as the foreign currency value of the inflow from abroad.

Private saving, $S_p$, is equal to income minus noninvestment expenditures, that is, consumption, taxes, and the transfer. Making the obvious substitution in (3) shows that net borrowing is equal to investment minus saving,

$$N_p=I-S_p.$$

Government net borrowing, $N_G$, is

$$N_G=G+Z_G-T, \tag{4}$$

with $Z_G$ as a transfer to the rest of the world (a negative quantity, $-eZ_G^*$, could stand for foreign aid, $Z_G^*$, arriving as foreign exchange in the form of a pure donation as opposed to a loan).

The rest of the world's net borrowing, $N_R$, is equivalent to the home country's acquisition of foreign assets or reduction of its foreign liabilities. The transaction has to take place via a surplus on the current account of the balance of payments,

$$N_R=E-eM^*-Z, \tag{5}$$

in which $Z=Z_p+Z_G$ (plus terms representing inflows if needed).

Let $N$ be total net borrowing. Assume by way of illustration that private and government net borrowing and the current account balance (rest-of-world net-borrowing flows) all depend on the level of output, $Y$. Then a key condition for macroeconomic balance is that

$$N(Y)=N_P(Y)+N_G(Y)+N_R(Y)=0. \tag{6}$$

When (6) is satisfied, running through the income-expenditure accounting shows that the "material balance" condition (2) will also hold.

Suppose that $Y$ initially satisfies (6) but then "blips" upward. If in response $N(Y)$ *decreases*, then the economy's total spending will fall short of income (total net borrowing becomes negative), and one would expect $Y$ to return to the level determined by (6). This sort of "counter-cyclical" response stabilizes the system. Of course, any one (or two) of $N_P$, $N_G$, or $N_R$ could respond positively ("pro-cyclically") to $Y$, but so long as $N(Y)$ goes down when $Y$ goes up, the economy will function.

When cumulated over time, net-borrowing flows generate balance sheets like the one presented in table 6.1. The time period relevant to the present discussion is the "short run," e.g., a month, a quarter, or at most a year.

To run through the accounting quickly, let a delta ($\Delta$) in front of a variable denote its change over time. The growth rate of, say, $X$ will then be $\Delta X/X$. Also note that the equity price index, $P_V$, and the exchange rate, $e$, are "asset prices" that can either "jump" in an instant or move steadily over time. Their growth or inflation rates are $\Delta P_V/P_V$ and $\Delta e/e$. Changes in wealth will depend on the corresponding capital gains or losses.

Investment (ignoring depreciation of existing capital and setting changes in inventories to zero) is equivalent to a change in the capital stock:

$$\Delta K = I.$$

The change in private wealth is equal to saving less capital losses on outstanding foreign loans or equity when $e$ or $P_V$ goes up,

$$\Delta \Omega_P = S_P - (\Delta e/e)eL_P^* - (\Delta P_V/P_V)P_V V.$$

The private sector's flow of funds is

$$N_P = I - S_P = \Delta(L_P + eL_G^*) + P_V \Delta V - \Delta(H + B_p).$$

Liabilities in the form of new loans and/or new issues of equity must go up or else holdings of money and government bonds decline when $N_P > 0$.

From the rest of the world's balance sheet in table 6.1, the home economy's net foreign assets are $-e\Omega_R^*$. Using (4), the *flow* change in the home country's foreign position can be written as

$$e(\Delta R^* - \Delta L^*) - P_V \Delta V_R = N_R = E - eM^* - Z.$$

Incorporating capital losses on loans and equity shows that

$$\Delta(-e\Omega_R^*) = N_R - (\Delta e/e)eL^* - (\Delta P_V/P_V)P_V V_R. \tag{7}$$

Equation (7) shows that on a *flow* basis a current account surplus is associated with growth in reserves and reductions in private and/or government external debt along with buying back home equity from abroad. As discussed in this chapter, if capital gains and losses are ignored, then from (7) the rest of the world's net foreign assets, $e\Omega_F^*$, in its T-account in table 6.1 will change only gradually over time. A consequence is that a "jump" upward or downward of foreign loans, $L_P^*$ or $L_G^*$, has to be met by a jump of (nearly) equal size in bank reserves, $R^*$. The same observation applies to a foreign equity purchase that increases, $V_R$, at the going price, $P_V$; in the first instance, the incoming funds will go into international reserves.

Three other flow-of-funds equations are also implicit in table 6.1. The simplest assumption for the banking sector is that its net borrowing, $N_B$, is equal to zero, which gives

$$N_B = \Delta H - \Delta(L + B_B + eR^*) = 0, \tag{8}$$

showing that the increase in the money supply (the banks' main liability) is equal to the sum of increases in loans to the private and financial sectors, holdings of government bonds, and international reserves. As with the foreign accounts, a jump in any item in the bank's T-account in table 6.1 has to be met by an offsetting jump on the other side of the balance sheet. For example, if reserves, $eR^*$, move upward, the money supply, $H$, has to do so as well (unless the banks sterilize the reserve increase by selling off government bonds, $B_B$).

The government's net borrowing takes the form of bond issues and higher foreign loans,

$$N_G = \Delta(B + eL_G^*).$$

The financial sector borrows from banks or abroad to buy up equity,

$$P_V \Delta V_F - \Delta(L_F + eL_F^*) = 0.$$

Capital gains in the form of $P_V > 0$ feed into an increase in financial wealth, $\Omega_P$, which can be plowed back into buying more equity "next period." Devaluation (an increase in the exchange rate, $e$) cuts into the financial sector's net worth, $\Omega_F$.

Finally, a quick look at determination of the exchange rate itself—the Mundell-Fleming and portfolio balance models, the trilemma, and how the rate may be set via its static and dynamic linkages with the rest of the system. Following Taylor (2004, 2008b), the main points are the following:

The Mundell-Fleming (or IS/LM/BP) model postulates three independent open economy macroeconomic relationships: (1) an IS curve to determine effective demand, (2) an LM to describe the financial system, and (3) a BP relationship to determine the current account. Output, the interest rate, and the exchange rate are supposed to adjust to equilibrate the three balances. But in fact equation (6) shows that if the economy is in macro equilibrium, the current account is already in equilibrium as well, for *any* value of the exchange rate.

An immediate corollary is that the trilemma does not hold. In a textbook world, the macro story needs to focus only on the level of activity and the interest rate. In the IS segment of the IS/LM/BP model, domestic and foreign incomes adjust to assure the equality in (6). So there is an open capital market, monetary policy is setting the interest rate (perhaps along an LM curve), and the exchange rate follows its own rules—the trilemma does not apply. The exchange rate (or some other variable such as the fiscal position) *would* have to become endogenous to allow (6) to balance if the current account were determined exogenously or by policy, but the trilemma is usually not presented in that way. The structural gap analysis in chapter 5 is a case in point.

Turning to portfolio balance involving stock variables as in table 6.1, three potential possibilities for closing a model are of interest. Each is counter-factual, illustrating the problems of applying simple models to functioning economies in real time.

In one possible closure, the monetary authorities in the home economy and the rest of the world intervene in markets to control their holdings of national and external bonds, and thus their money supplies at financial Stage II or higher. One can show that the interest rates in the two economies can adjust to clear their bond and money markets, independently of the exchange rate (there is no trilemma).[17]

A capital movement into the home economy represents a shift in foreign preferences away from foreign and toward home bonds. On standard liquidity preference grounds with constant money supplies, the home interest rate should decline and the foreign rate increase to reestablish local financial market equilibria. In fact, in many developing economies the interest rate went up after an inflow, suggesting that the authorities pursued contractionary monetary policy or that a strong increase in economic activity increased money demand.

In a second closure, the authorities fix interest rates as opposed to money supplies. This possibility is akin to inflation targeting as opposed to the first closure's traditional monetarist scenario. With fixed interest and exchange rates, asset demands as opposed to money supplies are now being held constant. After a capital inflow, money supplies must readjust to meet the constant demands—in other words, there will be automatic 100 percent sterilization of capital movements. Although in practice the authorities did attempt to sterilize in many countries, they were not completely successful because money supplies tended to increase after capital inflows. Again, a simple model closure misses the mark.

Finally, still assuming that the home country authorities are targeting the interest rate, they might *also* choose to hold reserves constant and allow the exchange rate to float. In this setup, one can show that through both wealth and substitution effects, the rate would decrease or appreciate after a capital inflow.

To summarize for emerging markets, the first closure suggests that an interest rate increase after a capital inflow must be attributable to restrictive monetary policy or higher economic activity. The second asserts that with pegged interest rates, there should be a degree of automatic sterilization after the inflow. But the third says it can't be complete because appreciation was often observed.[18] Insofar as simple short-run models apply, policy makers appeared to operate somewhere among the three closures.

In present circumstances in middle-income economies, it makes sense to go beyond static Mundell-Fleming or portfolio balance analysis and assume that a more-or-less floating rate is determined in spot and future asset markets. In effect, the spot rate floats against its "expected" future values. The quotation marks mean that we view expectations along Keynesian lines as emerging from diverse opinions on the part of market participants about how the rate may move.

A "speculative" view is that the exchange rate will *depreciate* when the local interest rate decreases. This view makes intuitive sense insofar as low interest rates should make national liabilities less attractive. It was perhaps first advanced macroeconomically by Minsky (1983). Recent macroeconomic history (Frenkel 2004) suggests that over the medium term, the speculative view is the more accurate description of exchange rate behavior in middle-income economies, that is, a high interest rate and a strong currency tend to run together.

## Notes

1. See Taylor (1994) for a brief history and an interpretation somewhat different from the one given in this chapter.
2. In Minsky's (1982) terminology introduced in chapters 1 and 6, the economy was engaging in Ponzi finance that was abruptly cut off.
3. In algebraic form, let $i$ be the local lending rate, $i^*$ the foreign borrowing rate, $\rho$ the risk premium, and $\hat{e}^E$ the expected rate of depreciation (the "hat" notation denotes a growth rate, $\hat{e} = (de/dt)/e$). Then interest rate arbitrage (usually called "interest rate parity" in the literature) as described in the text will give rise to the equation $i = i^* + \rho + \hat{e}^E$.
4. Note that we emphasize the *effect* of these swings in interest rates, which is procyclical. In traditional descriptions, interest rates are seen as counter-cyclical, in the sense that they move in the opposite direction to the business cycle (fall during booms, increase during crises).
5. In Brazilian 1950s slang "bossa" was more or less equivalent to the contemporary American "smooth." So inflation targeting is the newer, smoother Say's Law.
6. See John Taylor (1993). For all practical purposes, in the 1890s Wicksell proposed the same rule based on a "natural" interest rate.
7. See Barbosa-Filho (2008) and Galindo and Ros (2008).
8. The trilemma refers to the view that it is impossible to target simultaneously the interest and the exchange rates when the capital account is open. The standard references are Mundell (1963), Fleming (1962), and any textbook on open economy macro. Frenkel and Taylor (2007), Frenkel (2007), and Taylor (2008b) elaborate on these points.
9. In 2007, for example, foreign exchange reserve accumulation by developing countries was equivalent to 8 percent of GDP, out of which close to 6 percent of GDP originated in the capital account.

10. An additional reason for heavy interventions in foreign exchange markets is the "financial stability" motive (Obstfeld, Shambaugh, and Taylor 2008). The major argument is that financially open economies must hold reserves against capital flight, particularly the desire to convert domestic money balances (defined in a broad sense) into foreign exchange during crises. However, it is difficult to separate this motive from the "self-insurance" motive.

11. India's prior crisis in 1991 was caused by an unsustainable current account position under strict capital controls.

12. A similar case is borrowing by financial firms to acquire bonds issued in domestic currency by firms producing nontraded goods.

13. See, for example, Goodhart and Persaud (2008).

14. Other regulatory provisions can be used to discourage certain types of lending, for example, regulations on down payments for mortgages or the proportion of credit card lending that must be paid monthly.

15. One famous example involved major U.S. banks at the outset of the Latin American debt crisis. Many were technically bankrupt because the market value of their Latin American assets was very low. Regulators turned a blind eye, allowing the banks to carry the assets on their balance sheets at their value at maturity. This was good for the banks, as it avoided an open financial crisis, but it implied that the "solution" to the debt crisis was continuous debt renegotiations. The costs for Latin America were terrible: a lost decade for development. In a sense, Latin America paid dearly for the lack of transparency in the accounting of U.S. banks and the regulatory forbearance that was associated with it.

16. That is, as illustrated in the following, sectoral asset holdings from table 6.1 in the forms of money, bonds, or equity must be run down, and domestic or foreign loans must be run up.

17. This result is the open economy analog of the Stage II closed economy liquidity preference scenario in which a single interest rate adjusts to clear both bond and money markets.

18. Indeed, as noted previously, inflation targeting in emerging markets usually works by setting high interest rates to bring in capital inflows that lead to anti-inflationary exchange rate appreciation.

CHAPTER 8

# Growth and Sectoral Policy

POLICIES REGARDING GROWTH and sectoral strategies to support long-term structural transformation are the focus of this chapter. A theory of growth for a developing economy is the first topic. It serves as the background for analyzing policy frameworks for industry and agriculture and their interactions with trade.

## Growth Dynamics

Kaldor's (1978, chap. 4) model introduced in chapter 1 is the template for analysis of growth in the "modern" sector of the economy. We then turn to a "dual economy" extension simplified from Rada (2007).[1] The model is used to illustrate the implications of external liberalization packages à la the Washington consensus. A sketch of the supporting mathematics is given in appendix 8.1.

A basic assumption of this model is a significant underutilization (underemployment) of labor. Variations in the degree of underemployment together with the dynamic links between labor productivity and output, as established by the Kaldor-Verdoorn technical progress function, play the central role in growth dynamics. The Kaldor-Verdoorn mechanism that ties overall productivity growth to output expansion is essential to the model, and it captures both technical change that is "embodied" in new equipment and the increasing returns to scale of static and dynamic character that can be exploited or induced as the modern sector expands.

Under these conditions, demand plays a determining role in long-term growth, an issue generally ignored in the literature, which essentially focuses on supply-driven growth processes. The major exceptions are, or course, the Keynesian growth models developed in the 1950s and 1960s by Nicholas Kaldor (1978, chaps. 1 and 2) and Joan Robinson (1963), among others. Most of the macroeconomic dynamics analyzed by Lance Taylor (2004) fall under this tradition, taking particularly into account the links between the functional distribution of income and macroeconomic dynamics pioneered by Michal Kalecki.[2]

The model captures three essential features of growth processes in developing countries, which were presented in chapter 3. The first is that productivity growth is closely associated to dynamic structural change toward industry and modern services. The second is that variations in underemployment play an essential role in providing the labor force that facilitates the dynamic growth in the modern sector, but also serve to absorb the excess supply of labor when growth is weak. Variations in low-productivity informal services are the dominant mechanism of absorption of underemployment, as reflected in sharply diverging performance of labor productivity in service activities in different economies, but the rural sector still plays a role as an absorber of underemployment in many countries. The third feature is that capital accumulation is largely determined by demand—including in developing countries by external demand or constraints on domestic demand generated by the availability of external financing. It must be pointed out, however, that in dual economies, where a modern sector develops along with a low-productivity informal sector, productivity growth is always determined by the relative growth of the former, even if its growth is entirely supply driven (as in Ros 2000).

## Growth in the Modern Sector

The modern sector basically comprises industry along with parts of agriculture and services. It will be contrasted in this chapter with a "subsistence," or informal, sector with production assumed to rely on (low-wage) labor only. Following the discussion in chapter 1, the modern sector is characterized by increasing returns while constant or decreasing returns dominate subsistence.

The essentials of the model are presented in figure 8.1. An empirically well-supported relationship, usually credited to Kaldor (1978, chap. 4) and Verdoorn (1949), ties the rate of labor productivity growth to the rate of output growth. The rationale is that more rapid output expansion leads to introduction of more productive technologies and the realization of economies of scale both of static and dynamic character (learning-by-doing and induced innovations in the latter case). The Kaldor-Verdoorn elasticity of productivity growth with respect to output growth is usually estimated to be in the vicinity of 0.5. A natural extension of the relationship, not pursued in our discussion, is to assume that productivity also responds to the real wage, as firms react to rising labor costs. This linkage is empirically supported in industrialized economies (Naastepad 2006) but has not been explored in the development context.

**FIGURE 8.1**

## Kaldor model with (A) weak and (B) strong profit-led demand

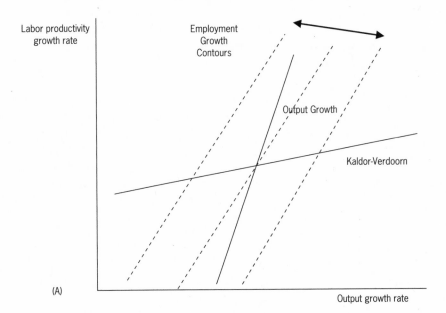

(A)

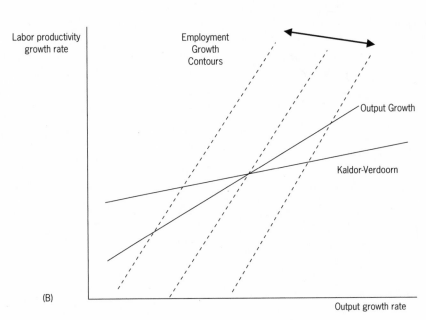

(B)

Kaldor also proposed that output growth would respond positively to productivity growth, as in the relevant schedules in diagrams. The usual justification follows from the definition:[3]

Unit labor cost = Real wage/Labor productivity

(given the level of aggregation, unit labor cost is also equal to the labor share in output). In a Keynesian economy in which output is determined by effective demand, what will be the effect of higher productivity? As emphasized by recent literature in structuralist macroeconomics (Taylor 2004), the answer can go both ways. On the one hand, it cuts unit labor cost and increases profitability, presumably stimulating exports and promoting capital formation. On the other hand, a lower labor share might be expected to reduce consumption and thereby effective demand. If the former effects dominate, the economy is said to be "profit led." If growth goes down with a reduction in the wage share, it is "wage led." Note that we are talking about *sufficient* conditions for an impact of productivity on demand and output growth. Other linkages are possible but have not been widely discussed.

The upper diagram (a) in figure 8.1 shows a case in which effective demand is *weakly* profit led. That is, with the steep output growth schedule, a big change in the productivity growth rate (vertical axis) does not stimulate much growth in demand. Demand is *strongly* profit led in the lower diagram (b), in which the output growth schedule has a shallow positive slope. Wage-led demand would generate an output growth curve with a negative slope.

An alternative (not formalized in the appendix 8.1) is to assume that the output growth relation is determined by foreign exchange constraints. In this case, the links between output and productivity growth operate through the effects that the latter has on the trade balance. To the extent that productivity growth in the modern sector leads to export expansion or the development of domestic import substitution industries, the slope of the output growth schedule is clearly positive, with the slope depending in this case on the response (elasticity) of the trade balance to productivity growth. The demand links formalized in the appendix will then enhance this effect (if the economy is profit led) or weaken it (if the economy is wage led).

The implications of different possibilities for employment can be visualized with the help of the employment growth contours, along which the employment growth rate stays constant. They are based on the identity:

Employment growth = Output growth − Labor productivity growth.

The definition implies that a given rate of employment growth can be generated by different combinations of output and productivity growth rates. Along each contour line (with a slope of unity, or 45 degrees), if the output growth rate is high, then productivity growth must be low and vice versa. Contours further to the southeast correspond to faster output expansion and therefore higher employment growth rates.

Now consider an upward shift in the Kaldor-Verdoorn schedule. In the upper diagram (a) the equilibrium point where the two schedules cross will move up from its initial position, signaling a slowdown in employment expansion or "jobless growth" with associated Luddite fears.[4] In the lower diagram (b), faster technical change gives rise to employment expansion as the equilibrium point moves below the initial output growth contour. The difference is that the elasticity of output growth with regard to productivity growth in the lower diagram is greater than one, so that the slope of the output growth schedule is less than 45 degrees. In other words, effective demand is strongly profit led when the elasticity exceeds unity; it is weakly profit led with an elasticity between zero and one; otherwise, it is wage led.

The Kaldor model strongly emphasizes potentially favorable effects of expansionary policy that shifts the output growth curve to the right. Regardless of the schedule's slope, the outcome is more rapid growth of both productivity and real (modern sector) GDP. The effects will be stronger insofar as domestic firms are open to innovation, as signaled by a steep Kaldor-Verdoorn curve.

We will use this model to explore likely impacts of liberalization packages, but to do so, we have to bring in an informal sector.

## The Dual Economy

There is a long tradition of studying a "dual" economy with two sectors having distinctive patterns of production. The approach has its roots in classical economics (especially Ricardo), as emphasized by W. Arthur Lewis (1954) in the most important modern contribution. It makes sense to combine Kaldor with a Lewis-style model in which labor *not* employed in the modern sector finds some sort of economic activity in "informal" or "subsistence" activities. A particular version of Say's Law thereby applies, as labor is "fully" employed, but its effects are attenuated by decreasing or at best constant returns in informal activities and an institutionally based gap between real incomes in the two sectors.[5] In reality, a large part of the labor force is *under*employed or, in Marxist language, the "reserve army" somehow finds the means for keeping itself alive.

How do they do it? Sharing subsistence-level production activity relying mostly on labor power is the obvious possibility. But then the question arises as to whether subsistence output will decline when some of the underemployed workers enter modern sector employment. Following Lewis, whether poor economies have reserves of "surplus labor" was hotly debated in the 1960s. Sen (1966) proposed that subsistence output would change by very little as labor moved in and out of the sector. In effect, his suggestion is that

Subsistence productivity = Subsistence output/Subsistence labor goes up in inverse proportion to the quantity of labor withdrawn, or that the elasticity of productivity with respect to the labor force is equal to minus one. This assumption boils down to a strong case of decreasing returns. Making use of a "Sen elasticity" ranging between zero (constant returns to scale) and minus one, we can now sketch a simplified version of the Kaldor-Lewis model put together by Rada (2007). The presentation here and in appendix 8.1 is simplified because we do not explicitly model shifting terms of trade between the two sectors. Implications are pointed out informally.

The framework is illustrated in the four-quadrant diagrams in figures 8.2 and 8.3. Along each of the four axes, the relevant variable is assumed to increase as indicated by the arrows. To concentrate on employment effects, the Kaldor part of the model is set up in the northeast quadrants of the diagrams with employment (instead of output) growth measured along the horizontal axes. Figure 8.2 illustrates the strongly profit-led case in which employment rises with faster productivity growth; the alternative scenario is shown in figure 8.3.

The task at hand is to trace the effects of shifts in employment growth on the subsistence sector and then close the loop back to the modern side of the economy. Modern sector equilibrium between employment and productivity growth rates is determined in the northeast (subject to the complication that demand for modern goods and associated jobs is likely to shift with subsistence

FIGURE 8.2

**Kaldor-Rada model with strong profit-led demand**

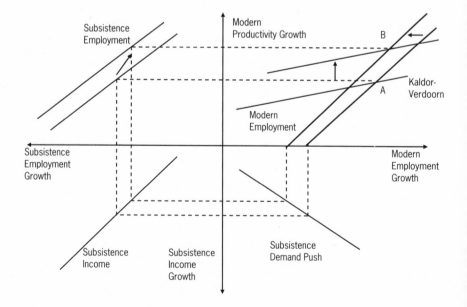

income). The next step is to derive subsistence sector employment growth in the northwest. A weighted average of the two employment growth rates must sum to the overall labor force rate of growth (the weights are the shares of the two sectors in total employment), which is assumed to be exogenous. The implication is that the subsistence employment growth rate falls when the modern sector rate rises.

The picture in the northwest involves a bit of algebraic manipulation (details in appendix 8.1) in that it links subsistence employment growth to modern sector *productivity* (not employment) growth. The trick works because employment and productivity growth rates in the modern sector are tied directly to one another in the Kaldor-Verdoorn relationship. The result is the subsistence employment schedule in the northwest quadrants, which show that subsistence employment growth speeds up when modern sector productivity growth drops off. As discussed later in this chapter, this dynamic works because the curve shifts outward when the Kaldor-Verdoorn schedule in the northeast shifts up.

Next, observe that *in terms of the subsistence product*, subsistence income growth is the sum of the sector's employment and productivity growth rates, as indicated by the subsistence income schedule in the southwest quadrants. The curve will be horizontal in the (extreme) Sen case in which income growth does not change in response to shifts in employment growth. It will have a slope of 45 degrees when there are constant returns to scale. For the curves sketched in the diagrams, the Sen elasticity is somewhere between zero and minus one.

Finally, assuming constant terms of trade, higher subsistence income growth will increase demand for modern sector goods as shown by the subsistence demand push in the southeast quadrant. The effect is apparent in the position of the intercept of the modern employment curve as it is determined by subsistence income growth.

Taking into account possible shifts in the terms of trade makes the analysis more complicated. Higher own productivity in the subsistence sector, for example, would increase own income but also bid down the price of its product. In Rada's model, depending on the price sensitivities of demand for modern goods from incomes in the modern and subsistence sectors, the slope of the subsistence demand push schedule can have either sign.

The diagram as drawn—with higher subsistence income stimulating demand despite the adverse shift in the terms of trade—is certainly plausible. But it runs counter to Malthus's position in the early nineteenth-century English Corn Law debates. He thought that grain price decreases induced by removing import quotas would be strong enough to drive down demand from the countryside for manufactures produced in the cities, leading to a "general glut" or overall stagnation. Malthus's position has resurfaced in a great deal of discussion about the impacts of agricultural productivity growth. As Houthakker (1976) pointed out in another model with explicit terms of trade, a sector (or an economy) selling its products into a price-clearing market with low elasticities of demand and supply enjoys no guarantee of rapid income growth.

The shifting curves in figure 8.2 show the effects of an upward movement of the Kaldor-Verdoorn schedule in the northeast quadrant from an initial equilibrium at point A. With a positively sloped modern employment schedule, the productivity gain stimulates labor force growth in the sector. Tracing the effect in the northwest, subsistence employment expansion slows (despite the outward shift of that curve, the growth rate of subsistence employment moves to the right on the horizontal axis). Subsistence income growth slows in the southwest, and tracing the repercussion through the southeast leads to a small leftward shift of the modern employment schedule in a final equilibrium at point B. In effect, the subsistence sector dampens the favorable impact of the modern sector productivity gain on employment growth.

Faster productivity growth in subsistence would shift the schedule "downward" in the southwest, increasing income growth. Tracing the effect along the subsistence demand push curve shows that the modern employment curve would move outward, triggering faster modern sector job growth, which would be scaled back a bit in a final equilibrium for the reasons just discussed. If adverse terms-of-trade effects create a "subsistence demand sink," these results on the impacts of productivity growth would reverse.

## A Low-Level Trap?

Figure 8.3 shows what happens when growth in the modern sector is weakly profit led or wage led, so that the employment schedule has a negative slope. An upward shift in the Kaldor-Verdoorn schedule from the initial equilibrium at A leads to slower employment growth in the modern sector. Tracing the effects through the subsistence sector shows a partially offsetting shift in the modern employment curve (weaker insofar as the Sen elasticity is closer to minus one) as the system arrives at a new equilibrium at B.

Figure 8.3 has implications for development policy. When productivity growth leads to slower employment growth in the modern sector, the economy can easily fall into a low-level equilibrium trap dominated by subsistence activities.[6] A coordinated policy package may be needed to get modern sector growth under way. China's gradualistic approach beginning in the late 1970s is an intriguing example. It began by supporting agricultural productivity growth through market manipulation to rig prices in favor of previously collectivized peasant producers. Joint ownership of land was retained with household-based operation of small and fragmented parcels. Mixed enterprises of various forms enabled mechanization and economies of scale. Producers responded strongly to the price incentives combined with institutional changes, which in effect amounted to a land reform.

FIGURE 8.3

## Kaldor-Rada model with weak profit-led or wage-led demand

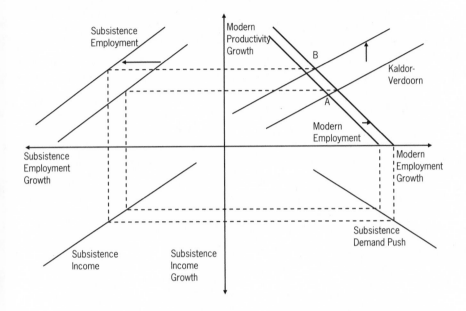

Subsequently, expansionary modern sector interventions combined with direct foreign investment to support export growth took center stage. A low-level trap was avoided, but distributive tensions are rising with modern sector incomes now growing much more rapidly than real earnings in the countryside.

In another example, if the modern sector mostly produces traded goods and subsistence produces nontradables, then the model sheds light on the liberalization experiences spurred by the Washington consensus. A de-industrialization trap can open.

As discussed in previous chapters, capital account deregulation was in many cases associated with real appreciation and domestic credit expansion. Together with trade liberalization, the stronger exchange rate boosted demand for imports and penalized exports (also hit by removal of subsidies in some cases). In figure 8.3 the impact was to shift the modern employment curve to the left. Offsetting influences were the credit expansion and rising private net borrowing during upswings. But even taking these factors into account, on the whole liberalization was not associated with a strong increase in demand for traded goods.

Traded goods firms were basically faced with a choice between cutting costs or going out of business. Boosting labor productivity was the most important way to keep production under way. On both counts, there was job loss as mirrored in an upward shift of the Kaldor-Verdoorn schedule. The scenario was like the one in figure 8.3, in some cases worsened by a leftward shift of the modern employment curve.

Unskilled workers bore the brunt of labor force reduction in traded goods, and shifted into informal and a range of subsistence activities. Distributive dynamics were driven by institutional circumstances in partly segmented labor markets, with details varying from country to country. In many cases, stable or rising unemployment and unresponsive wages caused the overall income distribution to become more concentrated. As has recently occurred in China, the differential between skilled and unskilled (and urban and rural) wage rates tended to rise.

The modern/traded goods sector in many developing economies across the world could have been supported by counter-cyclical policy, but for reasons discussed in chapter 7, this option was not aggressively pursued. Directed sectoral support policies could have been deployed but were ruled out by the non-interventionist prejudices of the Washington consensus. Nevertheless, policies oriented toward supporting production are still on the table.

## Industrial Policy

Historically and without exception, countries that have industrialized have, in a broad sense, pursued industrial policy. The American experience was briefly sketched in chapter 1, and the discussion could easily be expanded. For Britain, a long-standing tradition among economic historians emphasizes the role of fiscal expansion in support of military spending as the driving force behind post-Stuart output growth. An eminent practitioner observes that

> For more than a century, when the British economy was on its way to maturity as the workshop of the world, its governments were not particularly liberal or wedded ideologically to laissez-faire. Like the proverbial hedgehog of Aeschylus, the Hanoverian governments [1688–1815] knew some big things, namely that security, trade, Empire, and military power really mattered. In fruitful (if uneasy) partnership with bourgeois merchants and industrialists, they poured millions into strategic objectives which we can see (with hindsight) formed pre-conditions for the market economy and night-watchman state of Victorian England. . . . By that time men of the pen, especially the pens of political economy, had forgotten, and did not wish to be reminded, what the first industrial nation owed to men of the sword (O'Brien 1991, p. 33).

Chang (2002) and, more fundamentally, Polanyi (1944) argue that the Victorian state was not a night watchman but in fact quite interventionist. For

**FIGURE 8.4**

**Reducing unit labor costs by higher productivity or cutting wages**

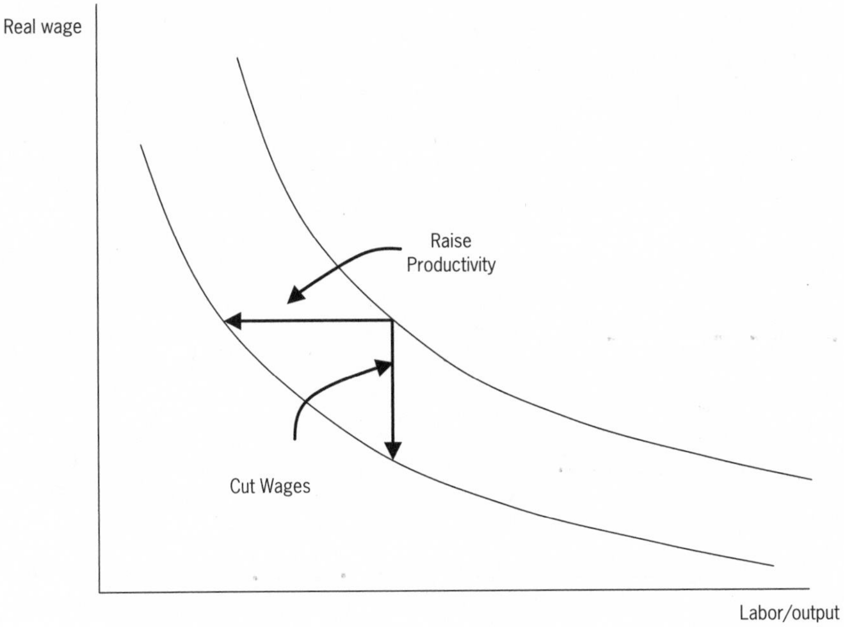

Real wage

Raise
Productivity

Cut Wages

Labor/output

present purposes that characterization is not the principal concern. The real interest lies with the pens of political economy, which on the whole have writ damnation on government interventions in industrial (and agricultural) economic activity, even though they are practiced universally. By advising endlessly about how to practice laissez-faire economic development, which in fact has never been observed, mainstream economists ignore practical policy considerations altogether. It makes sense to ponder what really happened on the ground. To make sense of the specific form of industrial policy pursued in many developing countries following World War II, it helps to start with a simple diagram proposed by Alice Amsden (2003). In figure 8.4, the definition of labor cost per unit output (slightly restated from above) is

Unit labor cost = Real wage × (Labor input/Output).

The curves represent the product of the real wage (vertical axis) and the labor/output ratio (horizontal) and are known as rectangular hyperbolae. A hyperbola lying further from the origin represents a higher level of unit cost. A firm or an economy operating at a high level of cost and striving to reach one that is lower has two extreme alternatives (or combinations thereof) open to it.

One is to cut wages and move cost vertically downward. The other is to increase labor productivity (decrease the labor/output ratio) and move horizontally to the left.

At a national level, a real devaluation (which could be accompanied to some extent by domestic inflation, due to the effects of the nominal exchange rate on domestic prices) is an effective means for reducing costs of exports as seen from abroad. Wage repression at home serves a similar function. But there may be social limits as to how far these measures can be pursued. If, given its *absolute* level of costs, a country is still unable to undersell its foreign rivals (as, say, South Korea could not undersell Japan in textiles in the 1950s), then the only option available is to stimulate productivity, usually through state intervention in the form of rigging internal import and export prices, directed and subsidized credit, and similar maneuvers (Amsden's famous recommendation to "get the prices wrong") in combination with performance standards dictated by the government to firms. "Administrative guidance" of industrialization is a useful summary phrase.

 A major institutional innovation in support of these polices was the creation of development banks. The banks were often funded "off" the fiscal budget by earmarked allocations or foreign borrowing and at their worst engaged in overlending. At their best, they were run by technocrats with the objective of building up technically advanced productive capacity. In economies lacking long-term capital markets, development banks became essential providers of funds for industrial investment.

The goals shared by the banks and other policy makers in a dozen or so middle-income countries in the 1950s were to induce firms to "learn" or acquire "specific assets" so that they could compete internationally, substituting imports and/or moving into export markets. Economies of scale were typically involved, raising a key issue of market regulation. There is an old idea in mainstream industrial economics that free entry of firms into an industry characterized by economies of scale is inefficient because too many potential producers come in to try to share the market, leading to a suboptimal level of investment by each one and prices too low to cover costs. Marxists use the label "excess competition" to describe this situation.

The implications are readily visualized in figure 8.5, similar to a diagram invented by the Swedish economist Eli Heckscher in 1918 to analyze the impact of tariff changes on industrial structure (Hjalmarsson 1991). Total production is measured toward the right on the horizontal axis, and time is measured toward the left.

At the far right, the dashed lines indicate the capacity (horizontal axis) and cost (vertical) of a production unit that recently has been scrapped. The unit is old. It is no longer in operation because its cost exceeds the current market price, determined by the cost of the still-functioning unit immediately to the left. Fur-

**FIGURE 8.5**

**Heckscher model of falling unit variable cost in newer production units**

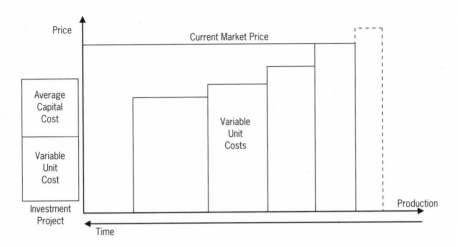

ther to the left comes a sequence of newer, larger, and less costly production units, with an even bigger one waiting as an "investment project" at stage left. If that project were activated on the basis of variable cost, it could undersell all preexisting units at a volume sufficient to cover its cost of capital. If *two* such units were to be put into production at roughly the same time, the industry in question would fall into excess competition, with older units forced out of production and perhaps with the new ones cutting price below variable cost to keep producing and covering capital costs.

In Sweden, Europe's industrial laggard until late in the nineteenth century, excess competition was mitigated by a "pro-trust" policy orientation, with tools such as tax exemptions used to encourage horizontal mergers between firms and vertical integration. Companies were actively encouraged to expand their market shares abroad, supported by Swedish direct foreign investment in many cases. One consequence is that Sweden now has a disproportionate share of successful transnational corporations.

In Asia 75 years later, competition policy was more hands-on. Planners set up devices such as investment regulation across firms, organization of cartels to keep firms in operation during periods of recession and downward international price excursions, and (when necessary) negotiated exit and capacity scrapping (Chang 1994). The more aggressive Asian policy is consistent with Gerschenkron's (1962) insight that state intervention tends to be more open and proactive, the more backward an economy attempting to industrialize is relative to the most developed countries.

Successful policy initiatives in "late (and late-late) industrializers" focused on *firms*, which were supposed to build up internal capabilities while attaining at least a minimum efficient scale of production. In the private sector, national leaders tended to be affiliates of a diversified industrial group with established government connections or a state spin-off. With direct public support, there was always a possibility of corruption and diversion of public funds into private pockets to the detriment of productive capacity in firms that may have become too large to be allowed to fail. In practice, governments could sidestep such problems of "moral hazard" by allowing *owners* of firms to go bankrupt, meanwhile keeping productive assets intact and transferring ownership rights to other entities.

Such maneuvers illustrate the basic nature of middle-income industrial policy as practiced in East and South Asia, Latin America, and Turkey but now, under the influence of the Washington consensus, largely abandoned outside Asia. Amsden (1989), Chang (1994), Wade (2003), and others describe a policy model based on mutual interactions—"reciprocal control mechanisms," to use Amsden's terminology—between selected firms as guided by the state's industrial bureaucracy. Firms received support for production in the form of import quotas and tariffs, export subsidies, direct allocation of cheap credit, etc. In exchange they had to satisfy specific performance criteria including quantitative targets for exports and volume of production and technological upgrading (monitored via indicators such as domestic content of the gross value of output). The goal of industrial policy makers was to make national production profitable, often at prices which were rigged toward that end. In Evans' (1996) phrase, these bureaucrats had enough "embedded autonomy" to be able to push their policies through. They were socially respected and upon retirement could expect an "ascent into heaven" paid for by firms they had helped create and build.

The interventions could be targeted quite specifically. Criteria for selection of industries to be supported included high-income elasticities of demand, strong production and technological linkages, economies of scale, and potential for productivity growth. Import protection was used to preserve the local market for national producers to finance the higher initial costs of the acquisition of technologies and associated learning processes. Export subsidies then promoted sales abroad from newly established production capacities and operated as a way to guarantee that producers were able to compete in international markets and manufacture world-class products. The fact that tariffs and subsidies, to an extent, were mutually offsetting did not mean that policy makers simply replicated a "level playing field" (as mainstream critics of industrial policy assert). Rather, the two instruments were used in tandem to enhance their distinct impacts. They also had the effect of promoting the production of import substitutes and exportable goods relative to nontradable goods and services, under the implicit assumption that growth and productivity effects were stronger in the tradables.

With ongoing productivity growth, real wages trended upward in the economies that kept up industrial growth over an extended period (in the recent period, they were mostly in Asia, as we saw in chapter 3). Consequently, new technologies and lines of production had to be brought in. Beginning in the 1980s, pro-trust policies began to be utilized to support industrial concentration, and national research and development efforts were expanded. In an interesting contrast, Asian economies focused more on building up national technological capability than did the Latin Americans, which relied more heavily on direct foreign investment in bringing in sophisticated lines of production. China, with its giant population with diverse levels of skill, is coming out somewhere in between but with increasing emphasis on building its own technological capability.

This distinction between strategies is relevant for countries with per capita incomes now in the range of hundreds or a few thousand dollars that have built up some manufacturing experience and have fairly sizable populations or good entrée into external markets. (The argument is that access to sufficiently large markets is essential to support production when there are economies of scale.) If successful, these economies will adopt some combination of the "Asian" and "Latin" models. Smaller countries always have more limited room to maneuver, but they can also develop different forms of intervention in their export sectors, to guarantee that in the long run they become an instrument for technological upgrading.

To a large extent, the traditional industrial policy tools previously described were dismantled in the developing world during the hegemony of the Washington consensus and would now have to be redesigned to fit the new restrictions imposed upon policy by the World Trade Organization (WTO). Tariff levels have been significantly reduced, quantitative import controls and "trade-related investment measures" (TRIMs) forbidden, and export subsidies severely constrained for middle-income countries (but subsidies for research and development and similar activities are still permitted). Intellectual property rights have become more stringent, closing the avenues long used by successful industrial and developing countries to copy technology, including reverse engineering. Low-income countries represent something of an exception because they have been granted the latitude to adopt active industrial and trade policies; nevertheless, many or even most do not use them, partly because they are constrained by conditionalities imposed in connection with international development assistance.

The idea behind Washington consensus/WTO policy was that free trade would do a better job at generating dynamic growth than industrial interventions. As we have argued extensively in this book, the evidence of development experience in recent decades does not support this claim. In a formal analysis of the econometric exercises used in the past to defend orthodoxy, Rodriguez and Rodrik (2001) and Rodriguez (2007) have shown that there is no empirical association between rapid economic growth and trade liberalization. As a matter of interest, this conclusion has been implicitly accepted in the World Bank's (2005, chap. 5) evaluation of trade reforms, which claim that openness to trade has been an ingredient of successful growth strategies. Note the subtlety: it is not trade *liberalization* that has done the job, but *openness to trade,* which, as the evaluation makes clear, can be the result of different trade strategies, many of them with strong elements of state intervention. In chapter 9, we will return to the debate on the design of industrial—or better, structural transformation policies—today.

## The Agrarian Question

The political economy of agriculture has vexed farmers, consumers, and the state since time immemorial. As previously noted, the sector's supply and demand elasticities are almost always low, meaning that prices can jump up and down rapidly, harming one or another important social group when they move either way.[7] Modern industrial development generates a big push to urban centers, leaving many rural areas behind, many of them dominated by existing or remnants of old social structures. The government gets caught in between and, for that reason, always intervenes heavily in agriculture.

For developmentalist purposes, it is helpful to think of agriculture as passing through three stages. The first two are of direct relevance to poor countries today.

The first is when land and labor productivity are very low, often accompanied in practice by highly exploitative forms of land tenure and extraction of "rents" or "surplus" from peasants and landless laborers. The issue at hand is how to get the sector moving, with ongoing productivity growth and rising incomes. In some historical cases—Japan after World War II and, in effect, China and Vietnam with their revision of collectivized systems in the 1970s and 1980s—land reform has been an important stimulus to growth.

During the second stage, with productivity growth under way, the crucial question is how the sector can be managed to support output and labor force growth throughout the economy, particularly to avoid large urban-rural and interregional inequalities from expanding.

The third stage is characterized by the fall of the share of food products in consumer budgets below, say, 30 percent, usually accompanied by a rapidly shrinking share of the labor force in agriculture. The most relevant question is then how to set the stage for a final "industrialization" of agriculture. The sector may not support the same standards of income as do urban industrial and service activities, and thus may become heavily subsidized, as is the rule in rich members of the OECD.

Insofar as such comparisons over vast reaches of time and space make sense, many poor countries today have agricultural productivity levels well below those of the prosperous OECD economies on the eve of their industrialization—no "agricultural revolution" has occurred. A 20 percent share of agricultural capital formation in the total might be a reasonable norm for those countries; the observed share in many is well less than 10 percent.

Further challenges to domestic agriculture are food aid and direct competition with heavily subsidized, highly efficient foreign producers under free trade agreements. The introduction of new, high-cost technologies by the state in alliance with foreign transnationals can push small landowners against the wall. Farmers around the world have been driven out of business by such pressures and, worst, driven to suicide, as has been the case for tens of thousands of Indian farmers beginning in the 1990s.

As with macroeconomics and industrial strategy, there are two broad approaches to agrarian policy—price fundamentalist and structuralist. The modern patron of the fundamentalist school was T. W. Schultz (1964), who wrote more or less directly in opposition to Arthur Lewis and provoked Sen's analysis of surplus labor discussed previously. In this mainstream view, the main causes of poor agricultural performance are distorted prices and lack of access to productive technology. The success of the Green Revolution thus came from generous price supports (on both inputs and output) for producers and the new high-yield technology.

Unmentioned are preconditions for the adoption of the seed-fertilizer-irrigation package and its side effects. The historical situation included a differentiated class structure in agriculture that allowed big "farmers" (almost in the American Middle Western sense of the word) to take advantage of decreasing costs implicit in mechanization, water control, and bulk deliveries of fertilizers and pesticides. State-provided irrigation infrastructure played an essential role.

Side effects included a worsening income distribution in the countryside, labor expulsion from farms, and the risks implicit in the adoption of monocultural cropping and dependence on ecologically damaging inputs. The main point is that agriculture is based on complex, well-established social structures that purely technocratic policy cannot take into account.

A more nuanced approach must confront this multitude of confounding factors: Technologically, extension of the area of cropped land will be difficult in many countries. Bangladesh, for example, now produces three crops of rice per year supported by widespread irrigation. In effect, its land area has been dramatically extended, but similar innovations will not be feasible in arid lands. The implication is that crop *yields* will have to rise to increase rural incomes.

Higher-yielding dryland crops, livestock disease control, small-scale water control, and other new technologies will be necessary, but they may be difficult to introduce. In an influential paper, Bhaduri (1973) pointed out that potential technological improvements may be thwarted by landlords who extract both rent and interest payments from their tenants.[8] Introduction of tube wells for irrigation in eastern India may well have been held back by such factors. Stagnation in backward agriculture is not limited to that corner of the world.

There are fiscal issues. Expanding public investment in rural infrastructure and providing subsidies where they are sensible is essential. But can agriculture be taxed to help underwrite expenditures to improve its performance? On the one hand, few countries are able to tax the sector effectively; on the other hand, higher crop production may enable a reduction in food subsidies.

External complications arise, especially with regard to trade. As mentioned previously, opening up low-productivity producers to external competition can be devastating. Probably 1.5 million Mexican maize farmers have been forced out of business since trade in the crop was opened under the North American Free Trade Agreement (NAFTA) in the mid-1990s. Ecological diversity has undoubtedly diminished in maize's homeland. Worldwide, local producers will be under threat if significant agricultural trade liberalization occurs under the ongoing but moribund Doha round of WTO trade negotiations.

As discussed previously, shifts in terms of trade and sectoral demand patterns can be crucial. Was Malthus correct in assuming that demand from agriculture supports industrial production, or would higher terms of trade choke it off by cutting real incomes in urban areas? The linkages can be quite complicated. Higher food prices harm landless laborers in India but help landed peasant producers in Anatolia.

In the long run, rising agricultural productivity must force the sector to adjust to falling terms of trade. A smooth decline would be desirable, avoiding destabilizing price shocks insofar as possible. Market intervention in the form of food storage and price regulation becomes almost inevitable. Nonprice incentives in agriculture also matter—e.g., good rural access to farm inputs and manufactured consumer goods, infrastructure, and other amenities.

Putting successful agrarian development packages together under all these constraints is not easy, but it has been done. Getting prices "right" (though not necessarily dictated by an unfettered market) can be an important component but by no means the only one. At times, technological advances are possible, as recently in Brazil where extensive liming and use of phosphorous fertilizers has permitted rapid yield increases in the previously barren Cerrado region in the west-central part of the country. As of mid-2008, with world food prices spiraling, putting together effective packages to raise agricultural productivity has assumed urgent importance.

# APPENDIX 8.1: THE KALDOR MODEL AND EXTENSIONS

Following Kaldor (1978, chap. 4), we set up a three-equation model for a modern sector of the economy (subscript $M$). Then following Rada (2007), we bring in a subsistence sector (subscript $S$) and consider how the two interact. For simplicity, we work in continuous time, with a "hat" over a variable signaling a rate of growth: $\hat{X}_M = \left(\dfrac{dX_M}{dt}\right)/X_M$.

As discussed in the text of this chapter, the first equation states that the growth rate of output, $\hat{X}_M$, in the modern sector responds inversely to the growth rate of the wage share, $\hat{\psi} = \hat{\omega} - \xi_M$, with $\omega$ as the sector's real wage and $\xi_M$ as its rate of labor productivity growth. The rationale is that higher profitability as signaled by the lower value of $\psi$ will stimulate investment and export growth,

$$\hat{X}_M = \hat{A} + \alpha(\xi_M - \hat{\omega}).\tag{1}$$

A negative $\alpha$ means that the aggregate demand is wage led. For $\alpha > 0$, it is profit led with productivity growth stimulating output growth. Demand is strongly profit led for $\alpha > 1$, in which case employment grows as well. The intercept term, $\hat{A}$, captures all other contributing factors to output growth, including growth of subsistence sector real income, $\hat{Y}_S$. To keep down notation, wage growth, $\hat{\omega}$, is set to zero in the following discussion.

As suggested by Kaldor (1978, chap. 4) and Verdoorn (1949), productivity growth is likely to respond to output growth,

$$\xi_M = \bar{\xi}_M + \gamma\hat{X}_M.\tag{2}$$

The Kaldor-Verdoorn elasticity, $\gamma$, usually takes a value of around 0.5 when it is estimated econometrically. The intercept term, $\bar{\xi}_M$, stands for a base rate of productivity growth.

Finally, we have an equation for the definition of productivity growth,

$$\xi_M = \hat{X}_M - \hat{L}_M,\tag{3}$$

with $\hat{L}_M$ as modern sector employment growth.

In figure 8.1, equation (1) is the output growth schedule, and (2) is the Kaldor-Verdoorn curve. The employment growth contours are based on (3).

Figures 8.2–8.3 for the Rada model are based on a rearrangement of equations (1)–(3) to set up modern sector dynamics in terms of employment and productivity growth rates. An initial equation for employment growth (in the northeast quadrant of the diagrams) is

$$\hat{L}_M = \hat{A} + (\alpha - 1)\xi_M.\tag{4}$$

Faster productivity growth increases employment growth only when aggregate demand is strongly profit led, or $\alpha > 1$. Zero productivity growth implies that $\hat{L}_M = \hat{A}$, so the intercept of the employment growth curve is on the horizontal axis in the $(\hat{L}_M, \xi_M)$, plane.

The Kaldor-Verdoorn schedule itself becomes

$$\xi_M = \frac{1}{1-\gamma}(\bar{\xi}_M + \gamma \hat{L}_M). \tag{5}$$

If we let $\sigma_M = \gamma/(1-\gamma)$, then $\sigma_M > 0$ signals increasing returns to labor use in the modern sector.

Let the total labor force be $L = L_M + L_S$, growing at a rate $n$. If $\lambda = L_M/L$, then growth rates of modern and subsistence sector employment trade off according to the equation

$$\lambda \hat{L}_M + (1-\lambda)\hat{L}_S = n.$$

Via (5) $\xi_M$ and $\hat{L}_M$ are related monotonically, so we can solve for employment growth in the subsistence sector as a function of $\xi_M$,

$$\hat{L}_S = \frac{1}{1-\lambda}\left[n + \frac{\lambda}{\gamma}\bar{\xi}_M - \frac{\lambda(1-\gamma)}{\gamma}\xi_M\right]. \tag{6}$$

This equation is the sectoral employment growth schedule in the northwest quadrant of figures 8.2–8.3.

The subsistence sector is subject to decreasing returns to scale, with labor as its only input. In the sector's analog to the Kaldor-Verdoorn equation, we have

$$\xi_S = \xi_S + \sigma_S \hat{L}_S, \tag{7}$$

with $\sigma_S < 0$ signaling decreasing returns to scale (in the text, $\sigma_S$ is Sen elasticity). Because the sector's real income growth is

$$\hat{Y}_S = \hat{L}_S + \xi_S = \bar{\xi}_S + (1 + \sigma_S)\hat{L}_S, \tag{8}$$

there would be strong decreasing returns for $\sigma_S = -1$ (the value proposed by Sen in the course of the 1960s debate over the meaning of subsistence agriculture). There would be constant returns for $\sigma_S = 0$. Equation (8) is the subsistence income growth curve in the southwest quadrant of figures 8.2–8.3.

Finally, subsistence income growth feeds back into modern sector employment according to a relationship such as

$$\hat{A} = \hat{B} + \eta \hat{Y}_S, \tag{9}$$

which is the subsistence demand push curve in the southeast quadrants.

## Notes

1. Simple, nonformalized versions of a similar model are also available in Ocampo and Taylor (1998) and Ocampo (2005).
2. See, in particular, the essays collected in Kalecki (1971).
3. We will use a slightly restated definition of unit labor cost in discussing industrial policy later in this chapter.

4. The term "Luddite" refers to the groups of workers in early nineteenth-century England who destroyed industrial machinery in the belief that its use diminished employment. It was coined after (the possibly mythical) Ned Ludd, a Leicestershire worker who originated the idea.

5. Neoclassically inclined development economists like to rationalize the gap using efficiency wage models and similar constructs, but here we simply take its existence for granted.

6. Rada (2007) works through the dynamics of how an economy can be caught in a low-level trap.

7. The price responsiveness of Chinese agricultural supply in the 1980s was exceptional, and surely linked to the institutional reforms put in place at the time.

8. In a nutshell, technological innovation may raise a tenant's income enough to allow him to pay off loans from the landlord. The potential loss of interest income induces the landlord to resist the innovation. Bhaduri's theory of agricultural stagnation remains highly controversial. Basu (1997) provides a useful summary from a sympathetic mainstream perspective.

# CHAPTER 9

# Stylized Facts and Policy Alternatives

THE MAIN OBJECTIVE of this book has been to explain why so many parts of the developing world have failed to generate stable rates of growth in per capita incomes, and to offer policy alternatives for them to correct this outcome. The failure of growth was particularly widespread during the quarter century or so after a series of adverse shocks beginning in the late 1970s. This period also coincided with a major shift in development policies toward an emphasis on market liberalization and a retreat from state intervention. History has not been kind to the mainstream interpretation of economic development and the policies associated with it.

We set ourselves the task of analyzing in chapters 2 to 5 the growth patterns of developing countries over the past several decades, based on a framework that emphasizes the role of economic structures set out in chapter 1. On the basis of this evidence, we provided in chapters 6 to 8 an alternative way to understanding financial structures, the macroeconomic dynamics of developing countries, and the challenges associated with the transformation of their production structures.

This chapter presents eight main stylized facts that can be drawn from our empirical analysis and, on the basis of this evidence, summarizes and in some cases expands our major policy conclusions. We also offer a contrast between the views that we develop in this book and mainstream analyses of growth.

## Stylized Facts

The first stylized fact that comes out from our analysis is that *convergence in income levels among countries is the exception rather than the rule*. This conclusion contrasts with the prediction of convergence—either in absolute or conditional form—that characterizes most orthodox models of economic growth. Indeed, divergent economic performance has been the major characteristic of the evolution of the income per capita between industrial and developing countries over the past two centuries. This phenomenon came back with force in the late 1970s, giving rise to a "great divergence" in the incomes of industrial and developing countries that characterized the last two decades of the twentieth century. This divergence was accompanied by very uneven growth among different developing countries, with the success stories of East and South Asia coinciding with the poor performance of most of the developing world.

The late twentieth-century divergence was associated with clustering of growth collapses (reduction in income per capita over several years), in sharp contrast to the clustering of success stories during both the postwar golden age and the recent 2003–2007 boom. The clustering in time of both successes and collapses underscores a second stylized fact: *international factors play a crucial role in the overall growth dynamics of the developing world.* Again, this finding contrasts with the emphasis on domestic policies and institutions as the basic determinant of economic growth that characterizes mainstream analysis and, in particular, its numerous massive cross-country econometric exercises (in which, with a few exceptions, international conditions are entirely absent from the analysis).[1]

2.

The high frequency of developing country growth collapses during the lost decade of the 1980s was associated with the unusually large and in a sense unprecedented interest rates and terms-of-trade shocks that they faced, the effects of which lasted until the early 2000s. The recent boom must be understood, in turn, as a result of the end of the long-term effects of these adverse shocks, together with the positive linkages generated by the new engines of the world economy, particularly China. In the case of several low-income countries, debt relief and increased aid also played a role. The rapid spread of the recent world financial crisis to the developing world in the second half of 2008 serves to reinforce this dependence of growth performance on international factors.

The painful adjustment and frustrating growth during the late twentieth century were accompanied with the change in the overall policy environment toward the Washington consensus emphasis on market liberalization. Fast-growing regions were less zealous about applying the liberalization philosophy, and performed better. Indeed, the clear success cases of the late twentieth century—various Tigers, China, and Vietnam among other countries in Southeast Asia, and more recently India—are hardly paragons of neoliberalism. They succeeded not because they followed, but rather because they deviated from widespread market liberalization of their economies, maintaining, in particular, crucial instruments of macroeconomic and industrial policies. Some Central and Eastern European policy makers think of themselves as neoliberal, but many vestiges of the old order, in the form of an industrial base and high levels of human capital, remain; their integration with the European Union was also a basic ingredient of their recovery from the transition crisis.

When looking at the domestic features of successful versus slow-growing economies in the developing world, a third stylized fact emerges, perhaps the most central to the analysis of this book: _structure matters._ When making this assertion, we rely on a large structuralist literature that, in different variants, goes back to Hollis Chenery and Raúl Prebisch, the two great intellectuals to whom this book is dedicated, as well as Karl Marx, Joseph Schumpeter, and Albert Hirschman, to mention just a few authors—by the way, of quite different ideological inclinations.

There is, again, a sharp contrast between this framework and most mainstream analyses, where production and trade structures are viewed as a passive outcome rather than an essential determinant of economic growth. There are exceptions to this rule, including leading developing economists critical of the Washington consensus (particularly Rodrik 2007), the neo-Schumpeterian growth literature (see, in particular, Aghion and Howitt 1998), and trade economists who have analyzed the implications of specialization patterns for growth and emphasize the diverse technological learning paths that characterize different economic activities (see, for example, Krugman 1987; Grossman and Helpman 1995). Our views share several of the analytical conclusions of these authors.

A large part of our analysis has precisely focused on figuring out just how and why structure matters. In the empirical decompositions of change in production structures, we saw that fast-growing economies are characterized by strong output and labor share shifts accompanied by sustained productivity growth, with strong reallocation effects in some cases. In contrast, in the less successful regions there was either scant structural change or deindustrialization combined with an increase in the share of informal, low-productivity services.

The analysis of trade structures likewise revealed that developing countries specialized in exports with high-technology contents tend to do better than those specialized in natural resourced-based exports, which tend to perform poorly. A similar story applies to trade in services. Successful economies, such as India, have specialized in dynamic services that contribute significantly to overall productivity growth and high skilled employment. In several other regions, tourism represented a dynamic service activity but lacked these productivity links.

This analysis carries an implicit message: intelligent sector-level policies can facilitate the development process. To an extent, structural change can be planned or, at least, induced.

This analysis sheds light on the determinants of productivity growth. Stated goals of the liberalization package were to enhance labor productivity and employment growth. Outside the consistently expanding economies, this goal was not achieved. Productivity movements across sectors differed in detail in the slow-growing and stagnant regions but, in general, did not add up to very much. Also, overall, liberalization did not help create jobs—industrial jobs in particular. Rather, it increased underemployment, which was absorbed most frequently in informal service activities and, in a few cases, in agriculture. The associated fall in productivity, which is quite common in the service sector in low-growth economies, indicates that poor productivity performance was more an effect than a cause of poor GDP growth.

This leads to a fourth stylized fact: *productivity growth is as much a result as a cause of economic growth, largely because demand matters not only for short-term but also for long-term growth.* This point is generally missed in most mainstream analyses of growth, which are essentially supply driven. The reason is that they assume full employment of available resources and the lack of any Kaldor-Verdoorn effects (or Arrow's "learning-by-doing"), in which production itself leads to productivity improvement.

The first of these factors is important, because the existence of a "reserve army or the underemployed" is a crucial structural feature of developing countries. Successful long-term economic performance is associated with the gradual absorption of the reserve army into the modern sector of the economy, whereas poor growth performance leads to the enlargement of the reserve army. The first linkage leads to an increase in overall productivity; the second to a reduction. Trying to understand these phenomena as some sort of "productivity shocks" simply misses the point emphasized previously: that productivity is both caused by and causes GDP performance.

The interactions of underemployment and Kaldor-Verdoorn effects are crucial to understanding the growth dynamics in developing countries. Even in purely supply-driven models, they give rise to the results predicted by classical development economists: possible low-growth traps and rapid growth as labor is dynamically allocated toward the modern sector (Ros 2000). More importantly for the analysis in this book, they generate a possible interaction between GDP and productivity growth in which growth is *demand led*. The relevant demand factor may be investment demand, as in the Keynesian growth models associated with Nicholas Kaldor and Joan Robinson. In developing countries, the most relevant factor may be an externally generated demand boom, in which favorable export and/or external financing conditions play the key role, amplified by their induced effects on domestic investment and consumption.

At a sectoral level, the dynamic economies of scale generated by the Kaldor-Verdoorn effects and by learning by doing are important in another sense: because they determine links between past and future patterns of specialization. Whether an economy is able to move toward higher value-added economic activities depends on the accumulation of technological capabilities, largely as a result of previous production experience. So, the capacity of the East Asian economies rapidly to transform their specialization patterns has been associated with their capacity to accumulate technological capabilities. But also, as we saw, the productive capacities built into Central and Eastern Europe as well as in the semi-industrialized economies during the era of more active state intervention gave them the possibility of diversifying their exports into mid-tech manufactures in the more open domestic and global environment of the late twentieth and early twenty-first centuries.

According to our empirical analysis, supply factors do not have the explanatory role assumed in the mainstream literature and, therefore, do not seem to have played the leading role in the success stories. There is a clear association between capital stock and output growth rates across all regions, but the supply-side interpretation is not compelling. The association can be better explained by rapid capital stock growth contributing to labor productivity growth and driving output growth from the side of demand with savings adjusting endogenously, rather than by higher savings leading to more capital that feeds into output via some sort of aggregate production function.

In turn, the other supply links generated by either human capital accumulation and opening economies to foreign direct investment are at best weak. Better nutrition, education, and health have an intrinsic value: they are human rights and merit goods. They may also play a more indirect role, as a "framework condition" for successful growth, but they do not seem to be a determinant of the varying performance of different developing countries or of changes in their momentum of economic growth through time (Ocampo 2005).

A supply-side interpretation is more appropriate for the changes in (fossil fuel) energy/labor ratios. The key policy question that arises is whether in the near future rich country energy/labor ratios can be reduced (or energy productivity increased relative to labor productivity) substantially by technological innovation and social rearrangements. If such innovations work out, then perhaps they can be passed to developing economies before the momentum of their population growth overwhelms all possibilities for combating global warming.

If there is a supply factor that plays a central role in developing country macroeconomic dynamics, it is foreign exchange availability rather than production capacity. This leads to a fifth stylized fact: *external shocks, both positive and negative, crucially influence the macroeconomic dynamics of developing countries.* Although related to the second stylized fact mentioned previously, this fact focuses on short-term GDP variations rather than on long-term growth dynamics. Counter-cyclical macroeconomic policies are key to coping with massive external shocks, not only to smooth the domestic impact of external demand fluctuations but also to prevent important macroeconomic prices— the exchange and interest rates, in particular—from deviating from their developmental objectives.

Avoiding exchange rate overvaluation during booms is crucial to support the structural transformation of the economies toward new export and import-competing sectors with higher technological content, and for export and production diversification in general. In turn, maintaining growth during externally induced crises requires both avoiding high interest rates and managing the foreign exchange constraint (the "external gap") faced by developing countries during these periods. Stability in both exchange and interest rates is also fundamental to facilitate rapid capital accumulation.

Regrettably, pro-cyclical macroeconomic policies have become the rule rather than the exception in the developing world. Pro-cyclical policy responses multiply the impacts of external shocks. The net result has been exchange rate appreciation and inflationary pressures during booms and severe recessions or outright growth collapses during crises. Liberalization policies may have helped to reduce inflationary pressures but have clearly worsened pro-cyclical responses through capital account and financial liberalization and their general disregard for the developmental objectives of exchange rate management.

Our sixth stylized fact is that *the dynamics of sectoral net-borrowing patterns strongly influence possibilities for macroeconomic management, but the dominant patterns are not those usually underscored in orthodox analyses.* Fiscal austerity packages implemented in many countries in the 1980s and the 1990s were supposed to lead to improvement in external balances along IMF financial programming lines. That clearly was *not* the common outcome. More typical were mirrored up-and-down co-movements of private balances and external borrowing. Financial deregulation and capital account liberalization strengthened this correlation, and were followed by financial crises in many countries, sometimes more than once. They help explain the erratic performances in several regions. Private and government balances sometimes moved in opposite directions, but this correlation has little to do with Ricardian equivalence and more with what the literature on binding external constraints predicts—including its traumatic manifestations in the face of foreign exchange scarcity, which includes inflation taxes and forced savings.

Macroeconomic flexibility, although difficult to define and even harder to attain, is certainly important. According to the analysis of sectoral gaps, the major task of counter-cyclical macroeconomic policies relates to the management of swings in private sector balances in the face of unstable external financing.

Structural conditions also matter in several ways. First, the character of developing countries as "risky borrowers" in international financial markets generates pro-cyclical variations in the availability of external finance and in "parity interest rates" (discussed in detail later in this chapter) that are very hard to manage, particularly when the capital account is fully liberalized. Also, some forms of trade specialization are more prone to macroeconomic shocks. In this regard, as we have seen, specialization in natural resource–based exports is more cyclically vulnerable than in manufacturing, and specialization in mid-tech manufactures (some of which have acquired commodity characteristics) is more cyclically prone than specialization in low- or high-tech manufactures.

7.    Additionally, *financial development plays a crucial role in both enhancing macroeconomic flexibility but also generates risks of its own.* This can be considered, indeed, as a seventh stylized fact. Financial development does increase the tools available for countries to manage boom-bust cycles. But it also generates the possibility of financial instability, which can have different characteristics, depending on the nature of the financial system. Prudential regulation and the diversity of financial intermediaries are critical to provide stability to the system.

8.    The previous seven lead to an eighth and final stylized fact: *success in the developing world is associated with States as much as markets.* States are responsible in particular for inducing a favorable structural transformation of the economy and for managing positive and negative external shocks. And, in both cases, the "policy space" provided by the international environment and international rule making is crucial. One of the most troublesome features of the more liberalized international and domestic environments that have prevailed in recent decades is that the policy space of developing countries has significantly shrunk.

After the failure of liberalization policies in inducing rapid growth in the developing world, a new sort of consensus has been developing in recent years that recognizes more explicitly the role of the state. Some of the elements of this new consensus are welcome, particularly its emphasis on social policy and infrastructure. The adverse effects of "pro-cyclical" macroeconomic policies are also increasingly being recognized. Indeed, the term "counter-cyclical" macroeconomic policies, long absent or mentioned only as a secondary issue in the mainstream literature, has made a strong comeback. But several of the active structural and macroeconomic policies that we emphasize in this book are still disregarded by the mainstream analysis. And the obsession with property rights has made the mainstream institutional literature "one dimensional," and incapable of understanding the positive links between state intervention and market success that underlies successful development experiences, in the industrial and developing world alike.

## Policy Alternatives

Myriad policy recommendations that are derived from our attempt to incorporate these stylized facts into our analytical framework are found throughout the book, particularly in chapters 6 to 8. In this section we recapitulate and in some cases expand on alternatives that should fit the characteristics of today's developing countries.

The core idea is that the success can be reproduced by other countries around the world if the policy agenda promotes changes in production and trade structures toward higher productivity sectors and utilization of idle resources, while at the same time it advances the development of financial structures and the adoption of counter-cyclical macroeconomic policies to manage both positive and negative external shocks. The policy space to adopt development and macroeconomic policies coherent with these objectives is crucial, as is overall policy coherence, particularly the coherence between short term macroeconomic management and developmental goals.

Patterns of transformation will not be necessarily the same everywhere. The level of development and, particularly, the degree of diversification of production and trade structures already achieved, the accumulated technological capabilities, the natural resource endowments, and the size of the economies are one set of structural factors relevant for choices in the area of production sector policies. The extent of financial development and the degree of integration into global financial markets are another set that will determine macroeconomic policy alternatives. More generally, the application of our framework must always be context specific, as it must take into account the specific structural features of a country and the international environment at a point in time. The mainstream search for "one size fits all" solutions that was so typical of Washington consensus policies is simply wrong. To have any chance for success, policy has to be tailored to each country's conditions and constraints.

## Macroeconomic Policies

In the macroeconomic area, the two crucial issues that we have underscored are the need to enhance financial development and to design appropriate counter-cyclical macroeconomic policies. There are others that we have not analyzed but are also crucial. Most important among them is the need to have an adequate and progressive tax base to facilitate the adequate provision of social services and social protection as well as infrastructure development.

Financial development implies, first, the development of a sound banking sector and domestic bond markets. In the latter area, central bank and government bonds are commonly the starting point, but the final objective should be the development of deep corporate bond markets that facilitate investment financing. When long-term funds for investment financing are not available, public sector or state-sponsored development banks can play a very important role. They continue to be important when commercial banks and corporate bond markets provide financing with only limited maturity. Development banks and state intervention in general can also play a role in increasing access to finance by agents that have limited access to financial markets, including small firms and poor households, particularly in the latter case for financing their major asset, housing.

As a matter of interest, state intervention is quite extensive in many of these areas even under highly sophisticated financial markets (for example, in the United States). The development of bond markets, stock markets, and other advanced forms of financing—such as sound securitized mortgages and sound derivative markets—may require the promotion of specific institutional investors, which operate as "market makers." Development banks, insurance firms, and pension funds play a role in these areas in many countries; specific state-sponsored agents do the same even in industrial countries (for example, in the case of the U.S. mortgage market).

The possibility of financial instability is present at all stages of financial development. Financial development has a dual effect in this area. On the one hand, a denser institutional network of financial agents can be stabilizing and broaden the policy space for counter-cyclical monetary policy. At the same time, however, new risks are created. They include maturity mismatches between investment requirements and available finance, currency mismatches when external liabilities are used to finance the acquisition of domestic assets (particularly those producing nontradable goods and services), excess leverage (the multiplication of financial liabilities relative to the capital base on which financial institutions operate), and even the sheer development of unsound financial instruments.

These risks are present in all financial systems as reflected, for instance, in the importance of the latter two in the recent financial crisis in the industrial countries, including collateralized debt obligations based on subprime mortgages and credit default swaps backed by very small capital bases. The first two sorts of risk are particularly important in developing countries, where variable mixes of maturity and currency mismatches are inherent to balance sheet structures.

Financial regulations must therefore become increasingly sophisticated as financial markets develop. Regulatory shortfalls are behind the high frequency of financial crises that have plagued the industrial and developing countries since the 1970s. Avoiding excess leverage and thus guaranteeing an adequate capital base in the financial system, as well as adequate provisions (or reserves) to cover expected losses, is the most basic issue. Almost equally important in developing countries is the management of maturity and currency mismatches. The simplest regulatory options are strict provisions or coverage for risk of balance sheets that have such mismatches, or quantitative limitations or even outright prohibitions on foreign currency borrowing by domestic agents that produce nontradable goods and services. And it should never be forgotten that over the centuries newly invented but unsound financial instruments have sparked many crises.

Finance is inherently pro-cyclical. Risks are accumulated during booms that are only evident at the end, when it is generally found that financial systems are seriously undercapitalized relative to the risks they have assumed. This recurring outcome lies behind a basic recommendation put forward in chapter 7:

prudential regulations should have a strong counter-cyclical component. One of the major problems behind current regulations is that they are actually pro-cyclical, including pro-cyclical patterns of credit ratings; the broad use of mark-to-market pricing, which fits transparency criteria but tends to transmit assets' boom-bust cycles to portfolios; risk evaluation models that because of their similar design, may actually turn markets more volatile; and, more broadly, the tendency to build excessive leverage and open speculative positions during booms. The simple recommendations are to increase capital or provisions for loan losses during booms, and to avoid mark-to-market asset pricing from feeding into leverage—by, for example, imposing limits during booms on the values of assets that can be used as a backing for credit or bond issues.

Pro-cyclical finance also calls forth counter-cyclical macroeconomic policies. The problem is that the pro-cyclical availability of external financing limits the space available to developing countries to adopt counter-cyclical policies. Fiscal policies can always play a role, for example, through progressive income taxes that would operate as an automatic stabilizer by increasing government revenues at a faster pace than overall economic activity during booms or temporary tax hikes during this phase of the business cycle, the design of permanent safety nets to support the vulnerable during crises, fiscal stabilization funds to "store" windfall revenues during upswings, and rules that target "structural" fiscal balances—i.e., a deficit adjusted by pro-cyclical swings in tax revenues and the costs of safety nets used as automatic stabilizers during crises. In practice, however, the application of these principles is difficult, largely because political pressures lead governments to spend during booms, particularly when they were forced to cut spending during the preceding crisis as part of orthodox stabilization packages. Thus, pro-cyclical fiscal policies are unfortunately a common pattern in the developing world—a trend that must certainly be reversed.

An even more problematic feature is the tendency of parity interest rates (the costs of external financing, including country risk spreads, plus expected depreciation, or minus expected appreciation, of the exchange rate) to fall during booms and increase during crises. If countries follow these trends, monetary policies will be pro-cyclical and exacerbate swings in output. But trying to increase interest rates during booms and reduce them during crisis, going against trends in parity rates, may simply worsen exchange rate instability. Indeed, higher rates during booms increases incentives to bring in more capital, reinforcing appreciation trends. Lower rates in a crisis can generate incentives to take capital out, thus enhancing exchange rate depreciation and the risks of recession or even a long period of foreign exchange scarcity if the economy has failed to diversify during the boom.

This sort of interaction is the true dilemma of monetary and exchange rate policies in open economies. Inflation targeting, the ruling paradigm of monetary policy, can provide a framework for counter-cyclical policies when domestic demand is the sole determinant of domestic prices. But its counter-cyclical effect is unclear when exchange rates are a major determinant of domestic prices and, in any case, by failing to set exchange rate or balance of payments objectives, it may result in excessive exchange rate fluctuations. As a short-run solution, exchange rate appreciation during booms will shift any excess demand toward the balance of payments. Although the inflation target may be met, the increase in the current account deficit and associated appreciation will become an element of vulnerability to a sudden stop in external financing. As a long-term solution, this choice entirely ignores the developmental dimensions of the exchange rate—that is, the links between the exchange rate and the diversification of the productive and trade structures.

Both from a short- and a long-term perspective, macroeconomic policies in developing countries should therefore include an element of "exchange rate targeting." (Frenkel and Taylor 2007; Frenkel 2007). The massive interventions in foreign exchange markets in developing countries in recent years means that they are also a "revealed preference" of economic authorities in many, if not most, countries.

The main contributions of macroeconomic policies to long-term growth are moderate and relatively stable long-term real interest rates and competitive and relatively stable real exchange rates. The first can facilitate investment financing. The second can contribute to structural change in the production and trade structures. The exchange rate becomes more important as the trade regime is liberalized because protection and export subsidies become less readily available to promote structural change. (This effect of trade liberalization has often been ignored.)

We have argued in this book that it is possible for macroeconomic authorities to set, within limits, *both interest and exchange rates*. In practice this freedom of maneuver may depend on a mix of capital account regulations and (possibly massive) interventions in the foreign exchange market. It is a rewarding exercise, as empirical evidence indicates, that exchange rate competitiveness has positive effects on economic growth in developing countries—or, what is a similar result, that a strong current account has positive effects, not only on short-term but also on long-term growth.

## Structural Transformation Policies

The major task of structural transformation policies is to facilitate a dynamic restructuring of production and trade toward activities with higher technological content. We argued that countries that have industrialized have, in a broad sense, always pursued industrial policies, a statement that applies historically to the United States and Great Britain as well as to Japan and the East Asian Tigers, among others. Industrial interventions have included trade policies (tariff and nontariff protection, and export subsidies) and tax incentives, but also "pro-trust" policies to help create national champions and the active utilization of military spending with industrialist objectives. The more aggressive East Asian policy in the post–Second World War period is, furthermore, consistent with Gerschenkron's (1962) insight that active state intervention tends to be more important for latecomers and, we could add, for late-latecomers.

The Washington consensus hit hard at these instruments and proposed that trade liberalization would be a less distortive and more powerful instrument of development. This proved to be wrong. As we have extensively argued in this book, trade liberalization has *not* been the instrument used by most of the successful developing economies, which have actively promoted the diversification of their production and exports toward sectors with higher technological content.

An appropriate integration into the world economy can, of course, be a powerful instrument of development policy. This concept has indeed always been at the heart of structuralist thinking. After all, according to the views of structuralists, the main objective of industrial policies was always to change the form of insertion of national economies into the global economic system— that is, to redefine the international division of labor, not to return to any form of "autarky" (a concept that is, in any case, irrelevant to understanding modern development). The real question is then, what are the instruments that developing countries can use to promote a better insertion into the world economy today.

In this regard, trade instruments are less readily available than in the past, except for low-income countries, and intellectual property provisions are more stringent. A major instrument that has *not* been limited by international agreements is development banking. In many successful experiences, state-supported banks have been a major channel for financing new developmental activities, mixed in several cases with some ingredient of state ownership. Some countries continue to use this mix, most notably China. In today's developing countries, government-backed long-term lending should be mixed with the encouragement of corporate debt markets, an activity that itself can be supported by development banks as "market makers."

Several criteria have been discussed on how to design industrial policies today (see, for example, Ocampo 2005; Rodrik 2007, chap. 4; World Bank 2005, chap. 5). As proposed in chapter 8, the objective of these policies should always be the promotion of patterns of structural change that lead to the accumulation of technological capabilities. On the basis of the ongoing debate, several criteria can be proposed.

The major one can be formulated in a straightforward way: policies should promote innovative activities that generate positive domestic spillovers. The concept of "innovative activities" should be understood in a broad sense, to refer not only to new technologies, but also new markets, new industrial structures, or exploitation of previously underutilized natural resources. In today's export-oriented developing countries, export diversification, in either products or markets, should certainly be a major objective. In all cases, we should emphasize that "innovation" is what is "new" for the country or region where it takes place, regardless of whether this activity is fully developed elsewhere. Domestic spillovers—production linkages and technological externalities—are critical to justify government action, as benefits should go beyond the firm that undertakes the innovation.

Implicit in the emphasis on spillovers is that state intervention should aim at higher "value added," either in terms of technological content or at least of domestic contents. Indeed, the latter follows from the fact that GDP is nothing else but value added. So, promoting pure assembly manufacturing or tourism with limited domestic contents is not desirable per se, unless that opens the space for further innovations down the line. It is perhaps paradoxical, as Rodrik (2007, chap. 4) has emphasized, that the major forms of "industrial policy" in recent decades have been the promotion of free trade zones and the attraction of direct foreign investment through tax breaks or full tax exemptions—that is, activities that tend to reduce rather than increase domestic linkages and value added.

In turn, the emphasis on "activities" rather than "sectors" raises a series of important questions. One is whether it is possible to separate an activity from the sector where it predominantly occurs. A particularly important case in this regard is whether it is possible to separate the process of promoting *production* from that of building *technological* capacities. The implicit assumption of old forms of industrial policy interventions was that the accumulation of technological capacities was closely tied to—in a sense, a by-product of—the development of particular sectors. Promoting increasingly sophisticated industrial sectors was, therefore, the way to both promote innovation and the accumulation of technological capacities. Technological advancement per se became a passive rather than an active process.

In today's world, the issue of whether to promote activities rather than sectors turns out to be a pragmatic question, of whether it is possible to de-link the innovative activity from the innovative sector. There is no single answer. But what is clear is that, whether a specific activity or a sector is promoted, and whether the "innovation" does not directly lie in the area of production (e.g., conquering new markets or exploiting new resources), what is essential is that the final goal is the accumulation of technological capabilities.

The emphasis on activities carries another message: as opposed to what was usually accepted in the past, sectors other than manufacturing also offer opportunities for innovation. They include modern services but also primary production, both in niche high-value-added products (e.g., fresh fruits and vegetables) and also the technological upgrading of other natural resource intensive activities.

This basic criterion applies at each stage of development, though in different ways, and opens possibilities of active policies for all countries. How to increase productivity in basic agricultural activities should be the starting point of any development policy in low-income countries. How to move from primary goods to resource based and low-skilled manufactures and services will be the challenge for low-income and low- and middle-income countries, while middle-income countries increasingly confront the choice of moving to manufactures and services with higher technological content. For those producing resource-based goods or mid-tech manufactures subject to strong cyclical swings, an important element of the strategy must be how to diversify toward less cyclically vulnerable export sectors and to accompany structural strategies with strong counter-cyclical macro policies.

Structural transformation involves a public-private partnership of some kind. The need for such a partnership is associated with the information problems that different agents face: better information of the private sector on production processes and specific markets, but better information of the state on the economy as a whole, on international conditions and processes and, of course, its capacity to enforce rules that benefit the whole of the private sector rather than individual agents. The nature of the partnership will vary from country to country, depending on the characteristics of both private agents and the state. In all cases, it should be understood as a mutual learning process.

The incentives that are designed may be horizontal (that is, an incentive that applies to a certain activity in all sectors) or selective. A preference for horizontal incentives may be correct in some cases, but they may be inadequate to promote the special activities that generate the strongest spillovers and associated accumulation of technological capabilities. When fiscal resources are involved, how to allocate them is always a selective decision, and it is better to adopt it on the basis of an explicit strategy.

Selective strategy is not just or even mainly about "picking winners"—the typical motto used by critics of industrial policies. Any success will involve a learning process, concentrating on what should be promoted and drawing lessons from making wrong choices. Individual firms in a free trade environment confront exactly the same the same problems.

The worst choice is for the state to assume that the task of designing appropriate structural development strategies is impossible and therefore to take a passive stance. Its appropriate strategy may be characterized as "discovering" or even "making winners" in close interaction with production sector firms. This emphasis follows from our basic framework of analysis; according to productivity, increases are, to a large extent, the result of production experience.

The decision-making process was no doubt simpler during the import substitution era, when it was based on what was imported and the size of domestic markets. For some export-oriented economies, looking at the export structures of countries with higher incomes may be appropriate. But, as industrializing economies (now South Korea, Taiwan, and in some aspects China) approach the world technological frontier, hands-on administrative guidance of the old style may not work (Woo 2007). However, even if the bureaucracy cannot foresee "the next big thing" in information or other new technology-oriented sectors, it can certainly help finance research and development, and provide long-term finance to firms and the infrastructure backup in these sectors—as in South Korea's 90 plus percent broadband Internet coverage. None of these policy areas is restricted by international agreements, and these types of policies are actively practiced by states in industrialized countries today.

Incentives should be matched by performance standards—"reciprocal control mechanisms," to use Amsden's (2003) terminology. They should be granted on a temporary basis and dynamically adjusted to move forward in the structural transformation process. But any a priori definition of the duration of incentives may turn out to be artificial and could lead to the loss of resources invested without the policy objectives being met. A much better solution may be designing a learning process that would lead to decisions about whether to dismantle failed policies or extend successful policies until they bear their full fruits.

Finally, all of this requires investing in institution building. The destruction of institutional capacity to pursue developmental policy area was devastating in most of the developing world under the Washington consensus. But nothing indicates that it cannot be rebuilt. Indeed, mainstream analysis usually carries a contradictory view regarding institution building. It is usually assumed that creating good central banks or tax authorities is within the reach of developing countries, but that promotion of productive sector development is somehow impossible. There is no reason for this assumption. Successful countries have shown that it can be done.

## International Environment

Although the focus of this book has been on domestic macroeconomic policies and structural development strategies, the international environment is critical, as clearly indicated by the clustering in time of successes and failures across a broad range of countries. So, designing better instruments for global macroeconomic policy management is essential for developing countries, as is their adequate voice and participation in the associated decision making.

Finally, and once again, international rule making should leave enough policy space for developing countries to adopt strategies and policies to manage external shocks and promote their structural transformation. This is an area where there has been a clear regression in recent decades. A more equitable world is certainly not a world based on rules that make development more difficult.

## Notes

1. See, for example, the well-known text of Barro and Sala-i-Martin (2003), where both the theoretical and the empirical literatures are summarized.

# References

Acemoglu, Daron and James A. Robinson (2005). *Economic Origins of Dictatorship and Democracy*. Cambridge, UK: Cambridge University Press.

Adrian, Tobias and Hyun Song Shin (2008). "Liquidity, Monetary Policy, and Financial Cycles," *Current Issues in Economics and Finance* (Federal Reserve Bank of New York), 14 (1): 1–6.

Aghion, Phillippe and Peter Howitt (1998). *Endogenous Growth Theory*. Cambridge, MA: MIT Press.

Akyüz, Yilmaz, ed. (2003). *Developing Countries and World Trade: Performance and Prospects*. Geneva: UNCTAD; Penang: Third World Network; London: Zed Books.

Alexander, Kern, John Eatwell, Avinash Persaud, and Robert Reoch (2008). *Financial Supervision and Crisis Management in the EU*. Strasbourg: European Parliament.

Amsden, Alice H. (1989). *Asia's Next Giant: South Korea and Late Industrialization*. Oxford, UK: Oxford University Press.

Amsden, Alice H. (2003). *The Rise of "The Rest": Challenges to the West from Late-Industrializing Economies*. New York: Oxford University Press.

Barbosa-Filho, Nelson H. (2008). "Inflation Targeting in Brazil: 1999–2006," *International Review Applied Economics*, 22 (2): 187–200.

Barbosa-Filho, Nelson H., Codrina Rada, Lance Taylor, and Luca Zamparelli (2008). "Cycles and Trends in US Net Borrowing Flows," *Journal of Post Keynesian Economics*, 30: 623–647.

Barro, Robert J. (1974). "Are Government Bonds Net Wealth?" *Journal of Political Economy*, 82: 1095–1117.

Barro, Robert J. and Jong-Wha Lee (2000). "International Data on Educational Attainment: Updates and Implications." Center for International Development Working Paper No. 42, Harvard University, April.

Barro, Robert J. and Xavier Sala-i-Martin (2003). *Economic Growth*. 2d ed. Cambridge, MA: MIT Press.

Basu, Kaushik (1997). *Analytical Development Economics*. Cambridge, MA: MIT Press.

Bhaduri, Amit (1973). "A Study in Agricultural Backwardness Under Semi-Feudalism," *Economic Journal*, 83: 120–137.

Braudel, Fernand (1979). *Civilization and Capitalism: 15th–18th Century*. 3 Vols. New York: Harper and Row.

Bridges, Hal (1958). "The Robber Baron Concept in American History," *The Business History Review*, 32: 1–13.

Chang, Ha-Joon (1994). *The Political Economy of Industrial Policy*. New York: St. Martin's Press.

Chang, Ha-Joon (2002). *Kicking Away the Ladder: Development Strategy in Historical Perspective*. London: Wimbledon.

Chang, Ha-Joon, ed. (2007). *Institutional Change and Economic Development*. London: Anthem Press.

Chenery, Hollis B. and Michael Bruno (1962). "Development Alternatives in an Open Economy: The Case of Israel," *Economic Journal*, 72: 79–103.

Coase, Ronald H. (1960). "The Problem of Social Cost," *Journal of Law and Economics*, 3: 1–23.

Collins, Randall (1980). "Weber's Last Theory of Capitalism: A Systemization," *American Sociological Review*, 45: 925–942.

Cramer, Christopher (2002). "The Economics and Political Economy of Conflict in Sub-Saharan Africa." In *Renewing Development in Sub-Saharan Africa: Policy, Performance and Prospects*, ed. I. Livingstone, pp. 55–80. London: Routledge.

D'Arista, Jane (2006). "The Implications of Aging for the Structure and Stability of Financial Markets." In *World Economic and Social Survey 2007*. New York: United Nations.

de Soto, Hernando (2000). *The Mystery of Capital: Why Capitalism Triumphs in the West and Fails Everywhere Else*. New York: Basic Books.

Diamond, Jared (1999). *Guns, Germs, and Steel: The Fates of Human Societies*. New York: W. W. Norton.

Easterly, William (2006). *The White Man's Burden: Why the West's Efforts to Aid the Rest Have Done So Much Ill and So Little Good*. New York: Penguin.

Evans, Peter (1996). *Embedded Autonomy: States and Industrial Transformation*. Princeton, NJ: Princeton University Press.

Ffrench-Davis, Ricardo (2006). *Reforming Latin America's Economies After Market Fundamentalism*. New York: Palgrave Macmillan.

Ffrench-Davis, Ricardo (2008). "From Financieristic to Real Macroeconomics: Seeking Development Convergence in Ees." Paper prepared for the Commission on Growth and Development. Available at http://www.growthcommission .org.

Fleming, J. Marcus (1962). "Domestic Financial Policies Under Fixed and Floating Exchange Rates," *IMF Staff Papers,* 9: 369–379.

Foley, Duncan K. (2003). "Financial Fragility in Developing Economies." In *Development Economics and Structuralist Macroeconomics,* ed. Amitava Krishna Dutt and Jaime Ros. Northhampton, MA: Edward Elgar.

Foley, Duncan K. and Thomas R. Michl (1999). *Growth and Distribution.* Cambridge, MA: Harvard University Press.

Frenkel, Roberto (1983). "Mercado financiero, expectativas cambiales, y Movimientos do Capital," *El Trimestre Económico,* 50: 2041–2076.

Frenkel, Roberto (2004). "Real Exchange Rate and Employment in Argentina, Brazil, Chile, and Mexico." Paper prepared for the Group of 24, Washington, DC, September.

Frenkel, Roberto (2007). "The Sustainability of Monetary Sterilization Policies," *CEPAL Review,* no. 93, pp. 29–36.

Frenkel, Roberto and Lance Taylor (2007). "Real Exchange Rate, Monetary Policy, and Employment." In *Policy Matters: Economic and Social Policies to Sustain Equitable Development,* ed. José Antonio Ocampo, Jomo K. S., and Sarbuland Khan, chap. 11. Hyderabad: Orient Longman; London: Zed Books; Penang: Third World Network.

Galindo, Luis Miguel and Jaime Ros (2008). "Alternatives to Inflation Targeting in Mexico," *International Review Applied Economics,* 22 (2): 201–214.

Gerschenkron, Alexander (1962). *Economic Backwardness in Historical Perspective.* Cambridge, MA: Harvard University Press.

Godley, Wynne and T. Francis Cripps (1983). *Macroeconomics.* London: Fontana.

Goodhart, Charles and Aninash Persaud (2008). "A Party Pooper's Guide to Financial Stability," *Financial Times,* June 4.

Grilli, Enzo R. and Maw Cheng Yang (1988). "Primary Commodity Prices, Manufactured Goods Prices, and the Terms of Trade of Developing Countries: What the Long Run Shows," *World Bank Economic Review,* 2: 1–47.

Grossman, Gene M. and Elhanan Helpman (1995). "Technology and Trade." In *Handbook of International Economics,* ed. Gene M. Grossman and Kenneth Rogoff, vol. 3, chap. 25. Amsterdam: Elsevier.

Hal, Bridges (1958). "The Robber Baron Concept in American History," *Business History Review,* 32 (1): 1–13.

Hausmann, Ricardo, Jason Hwang, and Dani Rodrik (2007). "What You Export Matters," *Journal of Economic Growth,* 12: 1–25.

Hirschman, Albert O. (1958). *The Strategy of Economic Development.* New Haven, CT: Yale University Press.

Hjalmarsson, Lennart (1991). "The Scandinavian Model of Industrial Policy." In *Diverging Paths: Comparing a Century of Scandinavian and Latin American Economic Development,* ed. Magnus Blomström and Patricio Meller. Washington, DC: Inter-American Development Bank.

Houthakker, Hendrik S. (1976). "Disproportional Growth and the Intersectoral Distribution of Income." In *Relevance and Precision: Essays in Honor of Pieter de Wolff*, ed. J. S. Cramer, A. Heertje, and P. Venekamp. Amsterdam: North-Holland.

Kaldor, Nicholas (1978). *Further Essays on Economic Theory*. London: Duckworth.

Kalecki, Michal (1971). *Selected Essays on the Dynamics of the Capitalist Economy*. Cambridge, UK: Cambridge University Press.

Keynes, John Maynard (1923). *A Tract on Monetary Reform*. London: Macmillan.

Keynes, John Maynard (1936). *The General Theory of Employment, Interest, and Money*. London: Macmillan.

Kindleberger, Charles P. and Robert Aliber (2005). *Manias, Panics, and Crashes: A History of Financial Crises*. 5th ed. New York: John Wiley.

Krugman, Paul (1987). "The Narrow Moving Band, the Dutch Disease and the Competitive Consequences of Mrs. Thatcher: Notes on Trade in the Presence of Scale Dynamic Economies," *Journal of Development Economics*, 27: 41–55.

Kuznets, Simon (1966). *Modern Economic Growth*. New Haven, CT: Yale University Press.

Josephson, Matthew (1934). *The Robber Barons: The Great American Capitalists, 1861–1901*. New York: Harcourt, Brace.

Lall, Sanjaya (2001). *Competitiveness, Technology and Skills*. Cheltenham, UK: Edward Elgar.

Lewis, W. Arthur (1954). "Economic Development with Unlimited Supplies of Labor," *Manchester School of Economics and Social Studies*, 22: 139–191.

Lindblom, Charles (1977). *Politics and Markets: The World's Political-Economic Systems*. New York: Basic Books.

Lucas, Robert E., Jr. (2000). "Some Macroeconomics for the 21st Century," *Journal of Economic Perspectives*, 14: 159–168.

Maddison, Angus (1995). *Monitoring the World Economy 1820–1992*. Paris: Organisation for Economic Co-operation and Development.

Maddison, Angus (2001). *The World Economy: A Millenial Perspective*. Paris: Organisation for Economic Co-operation and Development.

Maddison, Angus (2007). *Historical Statistics for the World Economy: 1–2003 AD*. Database hosted at the site of The Groningen Growth and Development Centre, at the University of Groningen, The Netherlands. Available at: www.ggdc.net/maddison/Historical_Statistics/horizontal-file_03-2007.xls.

Markowitz, Harry M. (1952). "Portfolio Selection," *Journal of Finance*, 7: 77–91.

Martinez-Alier, Juan with Klaus Schlüpmann (1991). *Ecological Economics: Energy, Environment, and Society*. Oxford: Blackwell.

McCarthy, F. Desmond, Lance Taylor, and Cyrus Talati (1987). "Trade Patterns in Developing Countries: 1964–1982," *Journal of Development Economics*, 27: 5–39.

McNeill, William (1976). *Plagues and Peoples*. New York: Doubleday.

Minoiu, Camelia and Sanjay G. Reddy (2007). "Aid Does Matter After All: Revisiting the Relationship Between Aid and Growth," *Challenge: The Magazine of Economic Affairs*, 50 (2): 39–52.

Minsky, Hyman P. (1975). *John Maynard Keynes*. New York: Columbia University Press.

Minsky, Hyman P. (1982). "The Financial Instability Hypothesis: A Restatement." In *Can "It" Happen Again? Essays on Instability and Finance*, chap. 5. Armonk, NY: M. E. Sharpe.

Minsky, Hyman P. (1983). "Monetary Policies and the International Financial Environment," St. Louis: Department of Economics, Washington University.

Mirowski, Philip (1989). *More Heat than Light: Economics as Social Physics, Physics as Nature's Economics*. Cambridge, UK: Cambridge University Press.

Moore, Barrington, Jr. (1966). *Social Origins of Dictatorship and Democracy: Lord and Peasant in the Making of the Modern World*. Boston: Beacon Press.

Mundell, Robert A. (1963). "Capital Mobility and Stabilization Policy Under Fixed and Flexible Exchange Rates," *Canadian Journal of Economics and Political Science*, 29: 475–485.

Naastepad, C. W. M. (2006). "Technology, Demand, and Distribution: A Cumulative Growth Model with an Application to Dutch Productivity Growth," *Cambridge Journal of Economics*, 30: 403–434.

Nayyar, Deepak (2005). "Development Through Globalization?" In *Advancing Development: Core Themes in Global Economics,* ed. George Mavrotas and Anthony Shorrocks. New York: Palgrave Macmillan.

North, Douglass Cecil (1990). *Institutions, Institutional Change, and Economic Performance*. Cambridge, UK: Cambridge University Press.

O'Brien, Patrick K. (1991). *Power with Profit: The State and the Economy 1688–1815: An Inaugural Lecture Delivered in the University of London*. London: University of London.

Obstfeld, Maurice and Kenneth Rogoff (1997). "The Intertemporal Approach to the Current Account." In *Handbook of International Economics,* ed. Gene M. Grossman and Kenneth Rogoff, vol. 3. Amsterdam: North-Holland.

Obstfeld, Maurice, Jay C. Shambaugh, and Alan M. Taylor (2008). "Financial Stability, the Trilemma, and International Reserves," NBER Working Paper 14217, August.

Ocampo, José Antonio (2005). "The Quest for Dynamic Efficiency: Structural Dynamics and Economic Growth in Developing Countries." In *Beyond Reforms, Structural Dynamics and Macroeconomic Vulnerability,* ed. José Antonio Ocampo, chap. 1. Palo Alto, CA: Stanford University Press and Economic Commission for Latin America and the Caribbean.

Ocampo, José Antonio (2008). "A Broad View of Macroeconomic Stability." In *The Washington Consensus Reconsidered*, ed. Narcis Serra and Joseph E. Stiglitz, chap. 6. New York: Oxford University Press.

Ocampo, José Antonio and Juan Martin, eds. (2003). *Globalization and Development: A Latin American and Caribbean Perspective.* Palo Alto, CA: Stanford University Press, Economic Commission for Latin America and the Caribbean, and World Bank.

Ocampo, José Antonio and Mariángela Parra (2003). "The Terms of Trade for Commodities in the Twentieth Century," *CEPAL Review,* no. 79, pp. 7–35.

Ocampo, José Antonio and Mariángela Parra (2007). "The Dual Divergence: Growth Successes and Collapses in the Developing World Since 1980." In *Economic Growth with Equity: Challenges for Latin America,* ed. Ricardo Ffrench-Davis and José Luis Machinea, chap. 4. Houndmills, Hampshire: Palgrave Macmillan and Economic Commission for Latin America and the Caribbean.

Ocampo, José Antonio and Lance Taylor (1998). "Trade Liberalization in Developing Economies: Modest Benefits but Problems with Productivity Growth, Macro Prices, and Income Distribution," *Economic Journal,* 108: 1523–1546.

Ocampo, José Antonio and Rob Vos, eds. (2008). *Uneven Economic Development.* Hyderabad: Orient Longman; London: Zed Books; and Penang: Third World Network.

Pasinetti, Luigi L. (1981). *Structural Change and Economic Growth.* Cambridge, UK: Cambridge University Press.

Podkaminer, Leon (2006). "External Liberalization, Growth and Distribution: The Polish Experience." In *External Liberalization in Asia, Post-Socialist Europe, and Brazil,* ed. Lance Taylor. New York: Oxford University Press.

Polak, J. J. (1957). "Monetary Analysis of Income Formation and Payments Problems," *International Monetary Fund Staff Papers,* 6: 1–50.

Polanyi, Karl (1944). *The Great Transformation.* New York: Rinehart.

Pomeranz, Kenneth (2000). *The Great Divergence: China, Europe, and the Making of the Modern World Economy.* Princeton, NJ: Princeton University Press.

Prebisch, Raúl (1950). *The Economic Development of Latin America and its Principal Problems.* New York: United Nations. Repr. *Economic Bulletin for Latin America,* 7 (1962).

Pritchett, Lant (1997). "Divergence, Big Time," *Journal of Economic Perspectives,* 11: 3–17.

Rada, Codrina (2007). "A Growth Model for a Two-Sector Economy with Endogenous Employment," *Cambridge Journal of Economics,* 31: 711–740.

Rada, Codrina and Lance Taylor (2006). "Empty Sources of Growth Accounting, and Empirical Replacements à la Kaldor and Goodwin with Some Beef," *Structural Change and Economic Dynamics,* 17: 486–500.

Ramsey, Frank P. (1928). "A Mathematical Theory of Saving," *Economic Journal,* 38: 543–559.

Reinert, Erik S. (2006). "Development and Social Goals: Balancing Aid and Development to Prevent 'Welfare Colonialism.'" In *Policy Matters: Economic and Social Policies to Sustain Equitable Development,* ed. José Antonio Ocampo, Jomo K. S., and Sarbuland Khan. New York: United Nations.

Robinson, Joan (1963). *Essays in the Theory of Economic Growth.* London: Macmillan.

Rodriguez, Francisco (2007). "Openness and Growth: What Have We Learnt?" In *Growth Divergence: Explaining Differences in Economic Performance,* ed. José Antonio Ocampo, Jomo K.S., and Rob Vos, chap. 7. Hyderabad: Orient Longman; London: Zed Books; Penang: Third World Network.

Rodriguez, Francisco and Dani Rodrik (2001). "Trade Policy and Economic Growth: A Skeptic's Guide to the Cross-National Evidence." In *NBER Macroeconomics Annual 2000,* ed. Ben S. Bernanke and Kenneth Rogoff, pp. 261–325. Cambridge, MA: National Bureau of Economic Research.

Rodrik, Dani (2007). *One Economics, Many Recipes: Globalization, Institutions and Economic Growth.* Princeton, NJ: Princeton University Press.

Ros, Jaime (2000). *Development Theory and the Economics of Growth.* Ann Arbor: University of Michigan Press.

Sachs, Jeffrey (2005). *The End of Poverty: Economic Possibilities for Our Time.* New York: Penguin.

Schultz, T. W. (1964). *Transforming Traditional Agriculture.* New Haven, CT: Yale University Press.

Sen, Amartya (1966). "Peasants and Dualism with or without Surplus Labor," *Journal of Political Economy,* 74: 425–450.

Sen, Amartya (2000). *Development as Freedom.* New York: Knopf.

Singer, H. (1950). "The Distributions of Gains Between Investing and Borrowing Countries," *American Economic Review,* 40: 473–485.

Singh, Ajit (1995). "Corporate Financial Patterns in Industrializing Economies: A Comparative International Study." International Finance Corporation Technical Paper No. 2, Washington, DC.

Smith, Adam (1776/2003). *The Wealth of Nations.* Repr. New York: Bantam Books.

Socolow, Robert H. and Stephen W. Pacala (2006). "A Plan to Keep Carbon in Check," *Scientific American,* 295 (3): 50–57.

Solow, Robert M. (1956). "A Contribution to the Theory of Economic Growth," *Quarterly Journal of Economics,* 70: 65–94.

Solow, Robert M. (1957). "Technical Change and the Aggregate Production Function," *Review of Economics and Statistics,* 39: 312–320.

Staritz, Cornelia (2008). Financial Structure, Investment, and Economic Development: A Flow of Funds Analysis for Emerging Countries. Ph.D. diss., New School for Social Research.

Stiglitz, Joseph and Bruce Greenwald (2003). *Towards a New Paradigm in Monetary Economics.* Cambridge, UK: Cambridge University Press.

Stiglitz, Joseph E., José Antonio Ocampo, Shari Spiegel, Ricardo Ffrench-Davis, and Deepak Nayyar (2006). *Stability with Growth: Macroeconomics, Liberalization and Development.* New York: Oxford University Press.

Syrquin, Moshe (1986). "Productivity Growth and Factor Reallocation." In *Industrialization and Growth*, ed. Hollis B. Chenery, Sherman Robinson, and Moshe Syrquin. New York: Oxford University Press.

Taylor, John B. (1993). "Discretion vs. Policy Rules in Practice," *Carnegie-Rochester Conference Series on Public Policy*, 39 (December): 195–214.

Taylor, Lance (1994). "Gap Models," *Journal of Development Economics*, 45: 17–34.

Taylor, Lance (2004). *Reconstructing Macroeconomics: Structuralist Proposals and Critiques of the Mainstream*. Cambridge, MA: Harvard University Press.

Taylor, Lance (2008a). "Energy Productivity, Labor Productivity, and Global Warming." In *Twenty-First Century Macroeconomics: Responding to the Climate Challenge*, ed. Jonathan M. Harris and Neva R. Goodwin. Northampton, MA: Edward Elgar.

Taylor, Lance (2008b). "A Foxy Hedgehog: Wynne Godley and Macroeconomic Modeling," *Cambridge Journal of Economics*, 32: 639–663.

Taylor, Lance and Codrina Rada (2007). "Can the Poor Countries Catch Up? Guarded Assessments on Mainstream Assumptions for the Early 21st Century," *Metroeconomica*, 58: 127–154.

Tilly, Charles (1992). *Coercion, Capital, and European States AD 990–1992*. Cambridge, MA: Blackwell.

UN-COMTRADE database. Free data access to more than 1 billion trade records starting from 1962 until 2008. Available at basehttp://comtrade.un.org/db/.

UNCTAD (2007). Handbook of Statistics 2006-2007 (Sales No. E/F.05.II.D.2, ISBN 92 1 012057-4), July, Geneva. Available at http://www.unctad.org/Templates/Webflyer.asp?intItemID=1397&docID=8612.

UNECA (United Nations Economic Commission for Africa) (2008). *2008 Economic Report on Africa*. Addis Ababa: United Nations.

United Nations (2007a). United Nations National Accounts Main Aggregates database 2007, United Nations Statistics Division.

United Nations (2007b). United Nations Commodity Trade Statistics database 2007 (UN-COMTRADE), United Nations Statistics Division.

United Nations (2007c). United Nations Common database (2007), United Nations Statistics Division.

United Nations (2008a). United Nations National Accounts Main Aggregates online database (2008), United Nations Statistics Division.

United Nations (2008b). United Nations Commodity Trade Statistics online database 2008 (UN-COMTRADE), United Nations Statistics Division.

United Nations Conference on Trade and Development (2007). *UNCTAD Handbook of Statistics, 2007.*

Verdoorn, P. J. (1949). "Fattori che Regolano lo Sviluppo della Produttivita del Lavoro," *L'Industria*, 1: 3–10.

Wade, Robert (2003). *Governing the Market: Economic Theory and the Role of the Government in East Asian Industrialization*, 2d ed. Princeton, NJ: Princeton University Press.

Woo, Meredith Jung-En (2007). "The Rule of Law, Legal Traditions, and Economic Growth: the East Asian Example." In *Institutional Change and Economic Development*, ed. Ha-Joon Chang. London: Anthem Press.

World Bank (2005). *Economic Growth in the 1990s: Learning from a Decade of Reform*. Washington, DC.

World Bank (2006). A New Database on Financial Development and Structure. Available at http://go.worldbank.org/X23UD9QUXo.

World Bank (2007). World Development Indicators Database 2007.Washington, DC.

World Trade Organization's Statistics database, covering merchandise trade by commodity from 1980 to 2008. Available at http://stat.wto.org/Home/WSDBHome.aspx?Language=E.

# Index